AMERICA'S FAVORITES™

Casseroles & One-Dish Meals

Publications International, Ltd.
Favorite Brand Name Recipes at www.fbnr.com

Pictured on the front cover: It's a Keeper Casserole *(page 54)*.

Pictured on the back cover *(left to right):* Creamy Chile and Chicken Casserole *(page 42)* and Hash Brown Casserole *(page 16)*.

ISBN-13: 978-1-4127-2234-6
ISBN-10: 1-4127-2234-9

Library of Congress Control Number: 2005924034

Manufactured in China.

8 7 6 5 4 3 2 1

Microwave Cooking: Microwave ovens vary in wattage. Use the cooking times as guidelines and check for doneness before adding more time.

Preparation/Cooking Times: Preparation times are based on the approximate amount of time required to assemble the recipe before cooking, baking, chilling or serving. These times include preparation steps such as measuring, chopping and mixing. The fact that some preparations and cooking can be done simultaneously is taken into account. Preparation of optional ingredients and serving suggestions is not included.

Contents

French Toast Strata

4 ounces day-old French or Italian bread, cut into ¾-inch cubes (4 cups)

⅓ cup golden raisins

1 package (3 ounces) cream cheese, cut into ¼-inch cubes

3 eggs

1 ½ cups milk

½ cup maple-flavored pancake syrup

1 teaspoon vanilla

2 tablespoons sugar

1 teaspoon ground cinnamon

Additional maple-flavored pancake syrup (optional)

1. Spray 11×7-inch baking dish with nonstick cooking spray. Place bread cubes in even layer in prepared dish; sprinkle raisins and cream cheese evenly over bread.

2. Beat eggs in medium bowl with electric mixer at medium speed until blended. Add milk, ½ cup pancake syrup and vanilla; mix well. Pour egg mixture evenly over bread mixture. Cover; refrigerate at least 4 hours or overnight.

3. Preheat oven to 350°F. Combine sugar and cinnamon in small bowl; sprinkle evenly over strata.

4. Bake, uncovered, 40 to 45 minutes or until puffed, golden brown and knife inserted into center comes out clean. Cut into squares and serve with additional pancake syrup, if desired.

Makes 6 servings

French Toast Strata

Mushroom & Onion Egg Bake

1 tablespoon vegetable oil

4 ounces sliced mushrooms

4 green onions, chopped

1 cup *each* low-fat (1%) cottage cheese and sour cream

6 eggs

2 tablespoons all-purpose flour

1/4 teaspoon salt

1/8 teaspoon black pepper

Dash hot pepper sauce

Preheat oven to 350°F. Grease shallow 1-quart baking dish. Heat oil in skillet over medium heat; add vegetables. Cook until tender; set aside. In food processor, process cheese until almost smooth. Add sour cream, eggs, flour, salt, black pepper and pepper sauce; process until mixed. Add vegetables. Transfer to prepared dish. Bake 40 minutes or until knife inserted near center comes out clean.   *Makes 6 servings*

6

Overnight Ham and Cheese Strata

12 slices white bread, crust removed

1 (10-ounce) package frozen chopped broccoli, thawed and drained

2 (5-ounce) cans HORMEL® chunk ham, drained and flaked

6 eggs, beaten

2 cups milk

1/4 cup minced onion

1/4 teaspoon dry mustard

3 cups shredded Cheddar cheese

Cut bread into small cubes. Layer 1/2 of bread cubes, broccoli and chunk ham in buttered 13×9-inch baking dish. Top with remaining bread cubes. Beat together eggs, milk, onion, and dry mustard. Pour over bread; sprinkle with cheese. Cover; refrigerate overnight. Heat oven to 325°F. Bake 55 to 60 minutes or until set.   *Makes 12 servings*

Mushroom & Onion Egg Bake

Spinach Sensation

1/2 pound bacon slices

1 cup (8 ounces) sour cream

3 eggs, separated

2 tablespoons all-purpose flour

1/8 teaspoon black pepper

1 package (10 ounces) frozen chopped spinach, thawed and squeezed dry

1/2 cup (2 ounces) shredded sharp Cheddar cheese

1/2 cup dry bread crumbs

1 tablespoon margarine or butter, melted

1. Preheat oven to 350°F. Spray 2-quart round baking dish with nonstick cooking spray.

2. Place bacon in single layer in large skillet; cook over medium heat until crisp. Remove from skillet; drain on paper towels. Crumble and set aside.

3. Combine sour cream, egg yolks, flour and pepper in large bowl; set aside. Beat egg whites in medium bowl at high speed of electric mixer until stiff peaks form. Stir 1/4 of egg whites into sour cream mixture; fold in remaining egg whites.

4. Arrange half of spinach in prepared dish. Top with half of sour cream mixture. Sprinkle 1/4 cup cheese over sour cream mixture. Sprinkle bacon over cheese. Repeat layers, ending with remaining 1/4 cup cheese.

5. Combine bread crumbs and margarine in small bowl; sprinkle evenly over cheese. Bake, uncovered, 30 to 35 minutes or until egg mixture is set. Let stand 5 minutes before serving. Garnish as desired.

Makes 6 servings

8

Spinach Sensation

Easy Morning Strata

 1 pound **BOB EVANS**® Original Recipe Roll Sausage
 8 eggs
10 slices bread, cut into cubes (about 10 cups)
 3 cups milk
 2 cups (8 ounces) shredded Cheddar cheese
 2 cups (8 ounces) sliced fresh mushrooms
 1 (10-ounce) package frozen cut asparagus, thawed and drained
 2 tablespoons butter or margarine, melted
 2 tablespoons all-purpose flour
 1 tablespoon dry mustard
 2 teaspoons dried basil leaves
 1 teaspoon salt

Crumble sausage into large skillet. Cook over medium heat until browned, stirring occasionally. Drain off any drippings. Whisk eggs in large bowl. Add sausage and remaining ingredients; mix well. Spoon into greased 13×9-inch baking dish. Cover; refrigerate 8 hours or overnight. Preheat oven to 350°F. Bake 60 to 70 minutes or until knife inserted near center comes out clean. Let stand 5 minutes before cutting into squares; serve hot. Refrigerate leftovers.   *Makes 10 to 12 servings*

Serving Suggestion: Serve with sliced fresh plums.

10

Easy Morning Strata

Asparagus Frittata Casserole

3 large eggs

1 ½ cups 1% milk

1 teaspoon salt

1 box (10 ounces) BIRDS EYE® frozen Deluxe Asparagus Spears, thawed

½ cup shredded Monterey Jack or Cheddar cheese

✦ Preheat oven to 400°F.

✦ In medium bowl, beat eggs. Add milk and salt; blend well.

✦ Pour mixture into greased 9×9-inch baking pan; top with asparagus.

✦ Sprinkle with cheese.

✦ Bake 15 minutes or until egg mixture is set.   *Makes 4 servings*

Prep Time: 5 minutes ✦ Cook Time: 15 minutes

12

Ranch Quiche Lorraine

2 cups crushed butter-flavored crackers

6 tablespoons butter or margarine, melted

2 cups shredded Swiss cheese

4 eggs

2 cups heavy cream

1 packet (1.2 ounces) HIDDEN VALLEY® The Original Ranch® Dressing
    with Bacon

1 tablespoon dehydrated minced onion

Preheat oven to 375°F. In medium bowl, combine crackers and butter. Press crumb mixture evenly into 10-inch pie pan or quiche dish. Bake until golden, about 7 minutes. Cool in pan on wire rack.

Increase oven temperature to 425°F. Sprinkle cheese over cooled pie crust. In medium bowl, whisk eggs until frothy. Add cream, salad dressing mix and onion. Pour egg mixture over cheese. Bake 15 minutes; *reduce oven temperature to 350°F* and continue baking until knife inserted into center comes out clean, about 20 minutes. Cool on wire rack 10 minutes before slicing.   *Makes 8 servings*

SPAM™ Hash Brown Bake

- 1 (32-ounce) package frozen hash brown potatoes, thawed slightly
- 1/2 cup butter or margarine, melted
- 1 teaspoon salt
- 1 teaspoon black pepper
- 1/2 teaspoon garlic powder
- 2 cups (8 ounces) shredded Cheddar cheese
- 1 (12-ounce) can SPAM® Classic, cubed
- 1 (10³/₄-ounce) can condensed cream of chicken soup, undiluted
- 1 1/2 cups sour cream
- 1/2 cup milk
- 1/2 cup chopped onion
- 1 (4.25-ounce) jar CHI-CHI'S® Diced Green Chilies, drained
- 2 cups crushed potato chips

Heat oven to 350°F. In large bowl, combine potatoes, melted butter, salt, pepper and garlic powder. In separate large bowl, combine cheese, SPAM®, soup, sour cream, milk, onion and green chilies. Add SPAM™ mixture to potato mixture; mix well. Pour into 2-quart baking dish. Sprinkle with potato chips. Bake 45 to 60 minutes or until thoroughly heated.   *Makes 8 servings*

13

Ham and Cheese Bread Pudding

1 small loaf (8 ounces) sourdough, country French or Italian bread, cut into 1-inch-thick slices

3 tablespoons butter or margarine, softened

8 ounces ham or smoked ham, cubed

2 cups (8 ounces) shredded mild or sharp Cheddar cheese

3 eggs

2 cups milk

1 teaspoon dry mustard

$^1/_2$ teaspoon salt

$^1/_8$ teaspoon white pepper

1. Grease 11×7-inch baking dish. Spread 1 side of each bread slice with butter. Cut into 1-inch cubes; place on bottom of prepared dish. Top with ham; sprinkle with cheese.

2. Beat eggs in medium bowl. Whisk in milk, mustard, salt and pepper. Pour egg mixture evenly over bread mixture. Cover; refrigerate at least 6 hours or overnight.

3. Preheat oven to 350°F.

4. Bake bread pudding, uncovered, 45 to 50 minutes or until puffed and golden brown and knife inserted into center comes out clean. Garnish as desired. Cut into squares. Serve immediately. *Makes 8 servings*

Hot Tip

When making a casserole, it's important to bake it in the proper size dish so that the ingredients cook evenly in the specified amount of time.

14

Ham and Cheese Bread Pudding

Hash Brown Casserole

6 large eggs, well beaten

1 can (**12** fluid ounces) **NESTLÉ® CARNATION®** Evaporated Milk

1 teaspoon salt

¹/₂ teaspoon ground black pepper

1 package (**30** ounces) frozen shredded hash brown potatoes

2 cups (**8** ounces) shredded cheddar cheese

1 medium onion, chopped

1 small green bell pepper, chopped

1 cup diced ham (optional)

PREHEAT oven to 350°F. Grease 13×9-inch baking dish.

COMBINE eggs, evaporated milk, salt and black pepper in large bowl. Add potatoes, cheese, onion, bell pepper and ham; mix well. Pour mixture into prepared baking dish.

BAKE for 60 to 65 minutes or until set.   *Makes 12 servings*

Note: For a lower fat version of this recipe, use 3 cartons (4 ounces *each*) cholesterol-free egg product in place of eggs, substitute NESTLÉ® CARNATION® Evaporated Fat Free Milk for Evaporated Milk and 10 slices turkey bacon, cooked and chopped, for the diced ham. Proceed as above.

Hash Brown Casserole

Egg & Sausage Casserole

1/2 **pound pork sausage**

  3 **tablespoons margarine or butter, divided**

  2 **tablespoons all-purpose flour**

1/4 **teaspoon salt**

1/4 **teaspoon black pepper**

1 1/4 **cups milk**

  2 **cups frozen hash brown potatoes**

  4 **eggs, hard-boiled and sliced**

1/2 **cup cornflake crumbs**

1/4 **cup sliced green onions**

✦ Preheat oven to 350°F. Spray 2-quart oval baking dish with nonstick cooking spray.

✦ Crumble sausage into large skillet; brown over medium-high heat until no longer pink, stirring to separate. Drain sausage on paper towels. Discard fat and wipe skillet with paper towel.

✦ Melt 2 tablespoons margarine in same skillet over medium heat. Stir in flour, salt and pepper until smooth. Gradually stir in milk; cook and stir until thickened. Add sausage, potatoes and eggs; stir until well blended. Spoon into prepared dish.

✦ Melt remaining 1 tablespoon margarine. Combine cornflake crumbs and melted margarine in small bowl; sprinkle evenly over casserole.

✦ Bake, uncovered, 30 minutes or until hot and bubbly. Sprinkle with onions.

Makes 6 servings

18

Egg & Sausage Casserole

Make-Ahead Breakfast Casserole

2 1/2 cups seasoned croutons

1 pound **BOB EVANS**® Original Recipe Roll Sausage

2 1/4 cups milk

4 eggs

1 (10 1/2-ounce) can condensed cream of mushroom soup, undiluted

1 (10-ounce) package frozen chopped spinach, thawed and squeezed dry

1 (4-ounce) can mushrooms, drained and chopped

1 cup (4 ounces) shredded sharp Cheddar cheese

1 cup (4 ounces) shredded Monterey Jack cheese

1/4 teaspoon dry mustard

Fresh herb sprigs and carrot strips (optional)

Picante sauce or salsa (optional)

Spread croutons on bottom of greased 13×9-inch baking dish. Crumble sausage into medium skillet. Cook over medium heat until browned, stirring occasionally. Drain off any drippings. Spread over croutons. Whisk milk and eggs in large bowl until blended. Stir in soup, spinach, mushrooms, cheeses and mustard. Pour egg mixture over sausage and croutons. Refrigerate overnight. Preheat oven to 325°F. Bake egg mixture 50 to 55 minutes or until set and lightly browned on top. Garnish with herb sprigs and carrot strips, if desired. Serve hot with picante sauce, if desired. Refrigerate leftovers.

Makes 10 to 12 servings

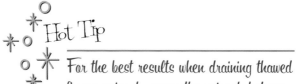

Hot Tip

For the best results when draining thawed frozen spinach, press the spinach between two nested pie plates, tilting the plates over the sink to drain well.

Make-Ahead Breakfast Casserole

Spinach and Cheese Brunch Squares

1 box (11 ounces) pie crust mix

1/3 cup cold water

1 package (10 ounces) frozen chopped spinach, thawed and well drained

1 1/3 cups *French's*® French Fried Onions

1 cup (4 ounces) shredded Swiss cheese

1 container (8 ounces) low-fat sour cream

5 eggs

1 cup milk

1 tablespoon *French's*® Bold n' Spicy Brown Mustard

1/2 teaspoon salt

1/8 teaspoon ground black pepper

Preheat oven to 450°F. Line 13×9×2-inch baking pan with foil; spray with nonstick cooking spray. Combine pie crust mix and water in large bowl until moistened and crumbly. Using floured bottom of measuring cup, press mixture firmly onto bottom of prepared pan. Prick with fork. Bake 20 minutes or until golden. *Reduce oven temperature to 350°F.*

Layer spinach, French Fried Onions and cheese over crust. Combine sour cream, eggs, milk, mustard, salt and pepper in medium bowl; mix until well blended. Pour over vegetable and cheese layers. Bake 30 minutes or until knife inserted into center comes out clean. Let stand 10 minutes. Cut into squares* to serve.

Makes 8 main-course servings

*To serve as appetizers, cut into 2-inch squares.

Prep Time: 20 minutes ✦ Cook Time: 50 minutes ✦ Stand Time: 10 minutes

Hint: The next time you make omelets, create onion omelets! Sprinkle French Fried Onions across the omelet before folding over. Enjoy!

22

Spinach and Cheese Brunch Square

Easy Crab-Asparagus Pie

4 ounces crabmeat, flaked
1 ½ cups sliced asparagus, cooked
½ cup chopped onion, cooked
1 cup (4 ounces) shredded Monterey Jack cheese
¼ cup (1 ounce) grated Parmesan cheese
Black pepper
¾ cup all-purpose flour
¾ teaspoon baking powder
½ teaspoon salt
2 tablespoons butter or margarine, chilled
1 ½ cups milk
4 eggs, lightly beaten

1. Preheat oven to 350°F. Lightly grease 10-inch quiche dish or pie plate.

2. Layer crabmeat, asparagus and onion in prepared dish; top with cheeses. Season with pepper.

3. Combine flour, baking powder and salt in large bowl. With pastry blender or 2 knives, cut in butter until mixture forms coarse crumbs. Stir in milk and eggs; pour over crabmeat mixture and cheeses.

4. Bake 30 minutes or until filling is puffed and knife inserted near center comes out clean. Serve hot. *Makes 6 servings*

Baked Ham & Cheese Monte Cristo

   6 slices bread, divided

   2 cups (8 ounces) shredded Cheddar cheese, divided

1 1/3 cups *French's*® French Fried Onions, divided

   1 package (10 ounces) frozen broccoli spears, thawed, drained and cut into
       1-inch pieces

   2 cups (10 ounces) cubed cooked ham

   5 eggs

   2 cups milk

   1/2 teaspoon ground mustard

   1/2 teaspoon seasoned salt

   1/4 teaspoon coarsely ground black pepper

Preheat oven to 325°F. Cut 3 bread slices into cubes; place in greased 12×8-inch baking dish. Top bread with 1 cup cheese, 2/3 cup French Fried Onions, the broccoli and ham. Cut remaining bread slices diagonally into halves. Arrange bread halves down center of casserole, overlapping slightly, crusted points all in one direction. In medium bowl, beat eggs, milk and seasonings; pour evenly over casserole. Bake, uncovered, at 325°F for 1 hour or until center is set. Top with remaining 1 cup cheese and 2/3 cup onions; bake, uncovered, 5 minutes or until onions are golden brown. Let stand 10 minutes before serving.   *Makes 6 to 8 servings*

25

Turkey-Tortilla Bake

9 (6-inch) corn tortillas
1/2 pound ground turkey
1/2 cup chopped onion
3/4 cup mild or medium taco sauce
1 can (4 ounces) chopped green chilies, drained
1/2 cup frozen corn, thawed
1/2 cup (2 ounces) shredded Cheddar cheese
Sour cream (optional)

1. Preheat oven to 400°F. Place tortillas on large baking sheet, overlapping as little as possible. Bake 4 minutes; turn tortillas. Continue baking 2 minutes or until crisp. Cool completely on wire rack.

2. Heat medium nonstick skillet over medium heat until hot. Add turkey and onion. Cook and stir 5 minutes or until turkey is browned and onion is tender. Add taco sauce, chilies and corn. Reduce heat and simmer 5 minutes.

3. Break 3 tortillas and arrange over bottom of 1 1/2-quart casserole. Spoon half the turkey mixture over tortillas; sprinkle with half the cheese. Repeat layers. Bake 10 minutes or until cheese is melted and casserole is heated through. Break remaining 3 tortillas into pieces and sprinkle over casserole. Garnish with sour cream, if desired.   *Makes 4 servings*

Prep and Cook Time: 30 minutes

Turkey-Tortilla Bake

Chicken & Biscuits

¼ cup (½ stick) butter or margarine

4 boneless skinless chicken breasts (about 1 ¼ pounds), cut into ½-inch pieces

½ cup chopped onion

½ teaspoon dried thyme leaves

½ teaspoon paprika

¼ teaspoon black pepper

1 can (about 14 ounces) chicken broth, divided

⅓ cup all-purpose flour

1 package (10 ounces) frozen peas and carrots

1 can (12 ounces) refrigerated biscuits

1. Preheat oven to 375°F. Melt butter in large skillet over medium heat. Add chicken, onion, thyme, paprika and pepper. Cook 5 minutes or until chicken is browned.

2. Combine ¼ cup chicken broth with flour; stir until smooth. Set aside.

3. Add remaining chicken broth to skillet; bring to a boil. Gradually add flour mixture, stirring constantly to prevent lumps from forming. Simmer 5 minutes. Add peas and carrots; continue cooking 2 minutes.

4. Transfer mixture to 1 ½-quart casserole; top with biscuits. Bake 25 to 30 minutes or until biscuits are golden brown.   *Makes 4 to 6 servings*

Hint: Cook the chicken in an ovenproof skillet and omit the 1 ½-quart casserole. Place the biscuits directly on the chicken and vegetable mixture and bake as directed.

Chicken & Biscuits

Classic Turkey Pot Pie

2 cans (15 ounces each) **VEG•ALL**® Original Mixed Vegetables, drained
1 can (10¾ ounces) condensed cream of potato soup, undiluted
¼ cup milk
1 pound (2 cups) cooked turkey, shredded
¼ teaspoon thyme
¼ teaspoon pepper
2 (9-inch) refrigerated ready-to-bake pie crusts

Preheat oven to 375°F. In medium mixing bowl, combine first 6 ingredients; mix well. Place 1 pie crust into 9-inch pie pan; pour vegetable mixture into pie crust. Top with remaining crust, crimp edges to seal, and slit top with knife. Bake for 50 to 60 minutes (on lower rack) or until crust is golden brown and filling is hot. Allow pie to cool slightly before cutting into wedges to serve.   *Makes 8 servings*

Turkey Broccoli Bake

1 bag (16 ounces) frozen broccoli cuts, thawed, drained
2 cups cubed cooked turkey or chicken
2 cups soft bread cubes
8 ounces sliced American cheese
1 jar (12 ounces) **HEINZ**® HomeStyle Turkey or Chicken Gravy
½ cup undiluted evaporated milk
   Dash pepper

In buttered 9-inch square baking dish, layer broccoli, turkey, bread cubes and cheese. Combine gravy, milk and pepper; pour over cheese. Bake in 375°F oven 40 minutes. Let stand 5 minutes.   *Makes 6 servings*

Classic Turkey Pot Pie

Enticing Enchiladas

1 tablespoon vegetable oil
1 green or red bell pepper, chopped
$1/2$ cup chopped onion
4 cloves garlic, minced
1 package **JENNIE-O TURKEY STORE**® Lean Ground Turkey
1 tablespoon Mexican seasoning or chili powder
2 cans (10 ounces) mild enchilada sauce
2 cups (8 ounces) shredded Mexican cheese blend or Monterey jack cheese
12 (7-inch) soft flour tortillas or flavored flour tortillas
1 cup shredded lettuce
$1/2$ cup diced tomato
   Ripe avocado slices (optional)

Heat oven to 375°F. Heat oil in large skillet over medium heat. Add bell pepper, onion and garlic; cook 5 minutes, stirring occasionally. Crumble turkey into skillet; sprinkle with seasoning and cook about 8 minutes or until no longer pink, stirring occasionally. Stir in $1/2$ cup enchilada sauce. Remove from heat; stir in 1 cup cheese. Spread $1/2$ cup enchilada sauce over bottom of 13×9-inch baking dish. Spoon about $1/3$ cup turkey mixture down center of each tortilla. Fold bottom of tortilla up over filling, fold in sides and roll up. Place seam side down in prepared dish. Spoon remaining enchilada sauce evenly over enchiladas. Cover with foil; bake 20 minutes. Sprinkle with remaining 1 cup cheese. Return to oven and bake uncovered 10 minutes or until cheese is melted and sauce is bubbly. Garnish with lettuce and tomato. Top with avocado, if desired.   *Makes 6 servings*

Prep Time: 30 minutes ✦ Cook Time: 45 minutes

Enticing Enchiladas

Coq au Vin

1/2 cup all-purpose flour
1 1/4 teaspoons salt
3/4 teaspoon black pepper
3 1/2 pounds chicken pieces
2 tablespoons butter or margarine
8 ounces mushrooms, cut in half if large
4 cloves garlic, minced
3/4 cup chicken broth
3/4 cup dry red wine
2 teaspoons dried thyme leaves
1 1/2 pounds red potatoes, quartered
2 cups frozen pearl onions (about 8 ounces)
Chopped fresh parsley (optional)

✦ Preheat oven to 350°F.

✦ Combine flour, salt and pepper in large resealable plastic food storage bag or paper bag. Add chicken, two pieces at a time, and seal bag. Shake to coat chicken; remove chicken and set aside. Repeat with remaining pieces. Reserve remaining flour mixture.

✦ Melt butter in ovenproof Dutch oven over medium-high heat. Arrange chicken in single layer in Dutch oven and cook 3 minutes per side or until browned. Transfer to plate; set aside. Repeat with remaining pieces.

✦ Add mushrooms and garlic to Dutch oven; cook and stir 2 minutes. Sprinkle reserved flour mixture over mushroom mixture; cook and stir 1 minute. Add broth, wine and thyme; bring to a boil over high heat, stirring to scrape up browned bits on bottom of Dutch oven. Add potatoes and onions; return to a boil. Remove from heat and place chicken in Dutch oven, partially covering chicken with broth mixture.

✦ Bake, covered, about 45 minutes or until chicken pieces are no longer pink in centers, potatoes are tender and sauce is slightly thickened. Transfer chicken and vegetables to shallow bowls. Spoon sauce over chicken and vegetables. Sprinkle with fresh parsley, if desired.

Makes 4 to 6 servings

Coq au Vin

Homestyle Chicken Pot Pie

2 tablespoons butter or margarine, divided

1 pound boneless skinless chicken breasts, cut into 1-inch pieces

$1/2$ teaspoon salt

$1/2$ teaspoon dried thyme leaves

$1/4$ teaspoon black pepper

1 package (16 ounces) frozen mixed vegetables, such as potatoes, peas and carrots, thawed and drained

1 can (10$3/4$ ounces) condensed cream of chicken or mushroom soup, undiluted

$1/3$ cup dry white wine or milk

1 refrigerated pie crust ($1/2$ of 15-ounce package), at room temperature

1. Preheat oven to 425°F. Melt 1 tablespoon butter in medium broilerproof skillet over medium-high heat. Add chicken; sprinkle with salt, thyme and pepper. Cook 1 minute, stirring frequently.

2. Reduce heat to medium-low. Stir in vegetables, soup and wine; simmer 5 minutes.

3. While soup mixture is simmering, unwrap pie crust. Using small cookie cutter, make decorative cut-outs from pastry to allow steam to escape.

4. Remove skillet from heat; top with pie crust. Melt remaining 1 tablespoon butter. Brush pie crust with 2 teaspoons melted butter. Arrange cut-outs attractively over crust, if desired. Brush cut-outs with remaining 1 teaspoon melted butter. Bake 12 minutes. Turn oven to broil; broil 4 to 5 inches from heat 2 minutes or until crust is golden brown and chicken mixture is bubbly.   *Makes 4 to 5 servings*

Prep Time: 5 minutes ✦ Cook Time: 25 minutes

Hint: If you skin and debone chicken breasts yourself, be sure to reserve both the bones and skin. Let these scraps collect in a plastic bag in your freezer and soon there will be enough to make flavorful homemade chicken stock.

Homestyle Chicken Pot Pie

Tex-Mex Ground Turkey Potato Boats

2 medium potatoes
1/2 **pound ground turkey**
1/2 **cup onion, chopped**
1 **clove garlic, minced**
1 **can (8 ounces) stewed tomatoes**
1 **teaspoon chili powder**
1/4 **teaspoon salt**
1/4 **teaspoon dried oregano leaves**
1/4 **teaspoon ground cumin**
1/4 **teaspoon red pepper flakes**
1/2 **cup (2 ounces) shredded reduced-fat Cheddar cheese**

1. Preheat oven to 400°F. Pierce potatoes several times with fork. Bake 50 to 60 minutes or until soft. Cool slightly. Reduce oven temperature to 375°F.

2. Slice potatoes in half, lengthwise. Scoop out pulp with spoon, leaving 1/4-inch shell. (Reserve potato pulp for other use.) Place potato shells on jelly-roll pan or baking sheet.

3. Place turkey, onion and garlic in medium skillet. Cook over medium-high heat 5 minutes or until turkey is no longer pink; drain. Add tomatoes, chili powder, salt, oregano, cumin and red pepper flakes to turkey in skillet. Cook 15 minutes or until most of liquid has evaporated.

4. Spoon turkey mixture evenly into potato shells; sprinkle with cheese. Bake 15 minutes or until cheese melts. *Makes 4 servings*

Favorite recipe from **National Turkey Federation**

38

Tex-Mex Ground Turkey Potato Boat

Turnip Shepherd's Pie

1 pound small turnips, peeled and cut into $^1/_2$-inch cubes

1 pound lean ground turkey

$^1/_3$ cup dry bread crumbs

$^1/_4$ cup chopped onion

$^1/_4$ cup ketchup

1 egg

$^1/_2$ teaspoon salt

$^1/_2$ teaspoon black pepper

$^1/_2$ teaspoon Beau Monde seasoning*

$^1/_3$ cup half-and-half

1 tablespoon butter or margarine

Salt and black pepper

1 tablespoon chopped fresh parsley

$^1/_4$ cup (1 ounce) shredded sharp Cheddar cheese

*Beau Monde is a seasoning salt available in most supermarkets. Celery salt can be substituted.

✦ Preheat oven to 400°F. Place turnips in large saucepan; cover with water. Cover and bring to a boil; reduce heat to medium-low. Simmer 20 minutes or until fork-tender.

✦ Mix turkey, bread crumbs, onion, ketchup, egg, salt and pepper. Pat onto bottom and side of 9-inch pie pan. Bake 20 to 30 minutes or until turkey is no longer pink. Blot with paper towel to remove any drippings.

✦ Drain cooked turnips. Mash turnips until smooth. Add half-and-half and butter; stir until well blended. Season with salt and pepper to taste. Fill meat shell with turnip mixture; sprinkle with parsley and cheese. Return to oven until cheese melts.

Makes 4 servings

Variation: For Rutabaga Shepherd's Pie, use 1 pound rutabagas in place of the turnips.

41

Turnip Shepherd's Pie

Creamy Chile and Chicken Casserole

3 tablespoons butter, divided

2 jalapeño peppers,* seeded and finely chopped

2 tablespoons flour

1/2 cup heavy cream

1 cup chicken broth

1 cup (4 ounces) shredded sharp Cheddar cheese

1 cup (4 ounces) shredded Asiago cheese

1 rib celery, chopped

1 cup sliced mushrooms

1 yellow squash, chopped

1 red bell pepper, chopped

12 ounces diced cooked chicken

1/4 cup chopped green onions

1/4 teaspoon salt

1/4 teaspoon black pepper

1/2 cup sliced bacon-Cheddar flavored almonds

*Jalapeño peppers can sting and irritate the skin; wear rubber gloves when handling peppers and do not touch eyes. Wash hands after handling.

1. Preheat oven to 350°F. For cheese sauce, melt 2 tablespoons butter in medium saucepan. Add jalapeño peppers; cook and stir over high heat 1 minute. Add flour; stir to make paste. Add cream; stir until thickened. Add broth; stir until smooth. Gradually add cheeses, stirring to melt. Set aside.

2. Melt remaining 1 tablespoon butter in large skillet. Add celery, mushrooms, yellow squash and bell pepper. Cook and stir over high heat 3 to 5 minutes or until vegetables are tender. Remove from heat. Stir in chicken, green onions, salt and pepper. Stir in cheese sauce.

3. Spoon mixture into shallow 2-quart casserole dish. Sprinkle with almonds. Bake 10 minutes or until casserole is bubbly and hot.   *Makes 6 servings*

Creamy Chile and Chicken Casserole

Sweet Potato Turkey Pie

1 can (24 ounces) sweet potatoes, drained

2 tablespoons margarine, melted

1/4 teaspoon pumpkin pie spice

   Nonstick vegetable cooking spray

2 cups cubed cooked turkey (1/2- to 3/4-inch cubes)

1 can (10 3/4 ounces) reduced-fat and reduced-sodium condensed cream of mushroom soup, undiluted

1 package (9 ounces) frozen French-style green beans, thawed and drained

1 can (2 ounces) mushroom stems and pieces, drained

1/2 teaspoon salt

1/2 teaspoon pepper

2 tablespoons crushed canned French fried onion rings

1 can (8 ounces) cranberry sauce (optional)

1. In medium bowl blend sweet potatoes, margarine and pumpkin pie spice until smooth. Spray 9-inch pie plate with cooking spray. Line pie plate with potato mixture to form a "pie shell;" set aside.

2. In medium bowl combine turkey, soup, beans, mushrooms, salt and pepper. Pour mixture into prepared shell. Sprinkle onions over top. Bake at 350°F 30 minutes or until hot. Serve with cranberry sauce, if desired.   *Makes 6 servings*

Favorite recipe from **National Turkey Federation**

Hot Tip

Substitute 1/8 teaspoon ground cinnamon, scant 1/8 teaspoon ground ginger and a pinch each ground allspice and ground nutmeg for 1/4 teaspoon pumpkin pie spice.

Sweet Potato Turkey Pie

Barbecue Chicken with Cornbread Topper

1 1/2 pounds boneless skinless chicken breasts and thighs, cut into 3/4-inch cubes

1 can (15 ounces) red beans, drained and rinsed

1 can (8 ounces) tomato sauce

1 cup chopped green bell pepper

1/2 cup barbecue sauce

1 package (6.5 ounces) cornbread mix plus ingredients to prepare mix

1. Heat nonstick skillet over medium heat. Add chicken; cook and stir 5 minutes or until cooked through. Preheat oven to 375°F.

2. Mix chicken, beans, tomato sauce, pepper and barbecue sauce in 8-inch microwavable ovenproof dish. Loosely cover mixture with plastic wrap or waxed paper. Microwave at MEDIUM-HIGH (70% power) 8 minutes or until hot, stirring after 4 minutes.

3. Meanwhile, prepare cornbread mix according to package directions. Spoon batter over chicken mixture. Bake 15 to 18 minutes or until toothpick inserted into center of cornbread layer comes out clean.

Makes 8 servings

Chicken Divan

3/4 pound fresh broccoli, cut into flowerets or 1 package (10 ounces) frozen broccoli flowerets

2 cups shredded cooked chicken

1 cup prepared HIDDEN VALLEY® The Original Ranch® Dressing

1 tablespoon grated Parmesan cheese

Cherry tomatoes

Preheat oven to 350°F. In medium saucepan, cook broccoli in boiling water to cover until tender, about 4 minutes. Drain thoroughly; place in shallow baking dish. Top with chicken and salad dressing. Sprinkle with Parmesan cheese. Cover loosely with foil; bake until heated through, about 15 minutes. Garnish with cherry tomatoes.

Makes 4 servings

Barbecue Chicken with Cornbread Topper

Hearty Chicken Bake

3 cups hot mashed potatoes

1 cup (4 ounces) shredded Cheddar cheese, divided

1 1/3 cups *French's*® French Fried Onions, divided

1 1/2 cups (7 ounces) cubed cooked chicken

1 package (10 ounces) frozen mixed vegetables, thawed and drained

1 can (10¾ ounces) condensed cream of chicken soup, undiluted

1/4 cup milk

1/2 teaspoon ground mustard

1/4 teaspoon garlic powder

1/4 teaspoon pepper

Preheat oven to 375°F. In medium bowl, combine mashed potatoes, 1/2 cup cheese and 2/3 *cup* French Fried Onions; mix thoroughly. Spoon potato mixture into greased 1 1/2-quart casserole. Using back of spoon, spread potatoes across bottom and up sides of dish to form a shell. In large bowl, combine chicken, mixed vegetables, soup, milk and seasonings; pour into potato shell. Bake, uncovered, at 375°F for 30 minutes or until heated through. Top with remaining 1/2 cup cheese and 2/3 *cup* onions; bake, uncovered, 3 minutes or until onions are golden brown. Let stand 5 minutes before serving. *Makes 4 to 6 servings*

Cheesy Turkey Veg•All® Bake

1 package (5 1/2 ounces) au gratin potato mix

2 2/3 cups boiling water

1 can (15 ounces) VEG•ALL® Original Mixed Vegetables, drained

1 cup cubed cooked turkey

2 tablespoons butter

Preheat oven to 350°F. Place au gratin potato mix and sauce packet into large mixing bowl. Add water, Veg•All, turkey, and butter; mix well. Pour into ungreased 2-quart casserole. Bake for 20 minutes or until top is golden brown. Cool for 5 minutes before serving. *Makes 6 servings*

Hearty Chicken Bake

Sour Cream Chicken Quiche

Crust

    Classic CRISCO® Single Crust (recipe follows)

Filling

    2 tablespoons CRISCO® Stick or 2 tablespoons CRISCO® all-vegetable shortening

    2 tablespoons chopped green bell pepper

    2 tablespoons chopped onion

    1 cup cubed cooked chicken

    1 tablespoon all-purpose flour

    ¼ teaspoon salt

    Dash nutmeg

    Dash black pepper

    ½ cup shredded sharp Cheddar cheese

    ¼ cup shredded Swiss cheese

    2 eggs, lightly beaten

    ¾ cup milk

    ¾ cup dairy sour cream

1. For crust, prepare as directed. Press into 9-inch pie pan. Do not bake. Heat oven to 400°F.

2. For filling, melt Crisco in small skillet. Add bell pepper and onion. Cook on medium-high heat 3 minutes, stirring frequently. Add chicken and flour. Cook and stir 2 minutes. Spread in bottom of unbaked pie crust. Sprinkle with salt, nutmeg and black pepper. Top with Cheddar cheese and Swiss cheese.

3. Combine eggs, milk and sour cream in medium bowl. Stir until smooth. Pour carefully over cheese.

4. Bake at 400°F for 20 minutes. *Reduce oven temperature to 350°F.* Bake 30 to 35 minutes or until knife inserted near center comes out clean. *Do not overbake.* Cool 10 minutes before cutting and serving. Refrigerate leftover quiche.

Makes 1 (9-inch) quiche

Classic Crisco® Single Crust

1 ⅓ **cups all-purpose flour**

½ **teaspoon salt**

½ **CRISCO® Stick or** ½ **cup CRISCO® all-vegetable shortening**

3 **tablespoons cold water**

1. Spoon flour into measuring cup and level. Combine flour and salt in medium bowl.

2. Cut in ½ cup shortening using pastry blender or 2 knives until all flour is blended to form pea-size chunks.

3. Sprinkle with water, 1 tablespoon at a time. Toss lightly with fork until dough forms a ball.

4. Press dough between hands to form 5- to 6-inch "pancake." Flour rolling surface and rolling pin lightly. Roll dough into circle. Trim circle 1 inch larger than upside-down pie plate. Carefully remove trimmed dough. Set aside to reroll and use for pastry cutout garnish, if desired.

5. Fold dough into quarters. Unfold and press into pie plate. Fold edge under. Flute.

6. **For recipes using a baked pie crust,** heat oven to 425°F. Prick bottom and side thoroughly with fork (50 times) to prevent shrinkage. Bake at 425°F for 10 to 15 minutes or until lightly browned.

7. **For recipes using an unbaked pie crust,** follow directions given for that recipe.

Makes 1 (9-inch) single crust

Easy Vegetable Beef Stew

1 pound beef for stew, cut into 1-inch pieces

1 can (14½ ounces) diced tomatoes, undrained

1 medium onion, cut into 8 wedges

4 carrots, cut into 1-inch pieces

1 green or red bell pepper, diced

1 rib celery, sliced

1 teaspoon dried Italian seasoning

½ teaspoon salt

½ teaspoon black pepper

1 tablespoon vegetable oil

1 package (8 ounces) sliced mushrooms

1. Combine beef, tomatoes with juice and onion in Dutch oven. Cover tightly; bake at 325°F 1 hour.

2. Add carrots, bell pepper, celery, Italian seasoning, salt and black pepper to beef mixture; stir. Cover; bake 45 minutes or until beef and carrots are tender.

3. Heat oil in large skillet over medium heat. Add mushrooms; cook and stir 10 minutes or until lightly browned and tender. Stir mushrooms into stew. Adjust seasonings to taste.

Makes 4 servings

Variation: Two unpeeled medium red potatoes, cut into 2-inch pieces, can be added with carrots.

Easy Vegetable Beef Stew

It's a Keeper Casserole

1 tablespoon vegetable oil
½ cup chopped onion
¼ cup chopped green bell pepper
1 clove garlic, minced
2 tablespoons all-purpose flour
1 teaspoon sugar
½ teaspoon salt
½ teaspoon dried basil leaves
½ teaspoon black pepper
1 can (about 16 ounces) whole tomatoes, cut up and drained
1 package (about 16 ounces) frozen meatballs, cooked
1 ½ cups cooked vegetables (any combination)
1 teaspoon beef bouillon granules
1 teaspoon Worcestershire sauce
1 can refrigerated buttermilk biscuits

1. Preheat oven to 400°F. Heat oil in large saucepan. Cook and stir onion, bell pepper and garlic over medium heat until vegetables are tender.

2. Stir in flour, sugar, salt, basil and black pepper. Slowly blend in tomatoes, meatballs, vegetables, bouillon and Worcestershire sauce. Cook and stir until slightly thickened and bubbling; pour into 2-quart casserole.

3. Unroll biscuits; place on top of casserole. Bake, uncovered, 15 minutes or until biscuits are golden.   *Makes 4 servings*

It's a Keeper Casserole

Mexicali Cornbread Casserole

2 ½ cups frozen mixed vegetables, thawed
1 ½ cups cubed **HILLSHIRE FARM®** Ham
1 package (10 ounces) cornbread stuffing mix
2 cups milk
3 eggs, lightly beaten
Salt and black pepper to taste
½ cup (2 ounces) shredded taco-flavored cheese

Preheat oven to 375°F.

Combine mixed vegetables, Ham and stuffing mix in small casserole; set aside. Combine milk, eggs, salt and pepper in medium bowl; pour over ham mixture. Bake, covered, 45 minutes. Top with cheese; bake, uncovered, 3 minutes or until cheese is melted.

Makes 4 servings

Pork Chops and Yams

4 pork chops (½ inch thick)
2 tablespoons **CRISCO®** Oil
2 (16-ounce) cans yams or sweet potatoes, drained
¾ cup **SMUCKER'S®** Orange Marmalade or Apricot Preserves
½ large green bell pepper, cut into strips
2 tablespoons minced onion

1. Brown pork chops in oil over medium heat.

2. Place yams in 1 ½-quart casserole. Stir in marmalade, bell pepper and onion. Layer pork chops over yam mixture. Cover and bake at 350°F for 30 minutes or until pork chops are tender.

Makes 4 servings

Mexicali Cornbread Casserole

Three Bean and Franks Bake

- 1 tablespoon vegetable oil
- 1 medium onion, chopped
- 2 cloves garlic, minced
- 1 red bell pepper, seeded and coarsely chopped
- 1 green bell pepper, seeded and coarsely chopped
- 1 can (16 ounces) vegetarian baked beans
- 1 can (16 ounces) butter or lima beans, drained
- 1 can (16 ounces) red or kidney beans, drained
- 1/2 cup packed light brown sugar
- 1/2 cup ketchup
- 2 tablespoons cider vinegar
- 1 tablespoon **HEBREW NATIONAL®** Deli Mustard
- 1 package (12 ounces) **HEBREW NATIONAL®** Beef Franks, Reduced Fat Beef Franks or 97% Fat Free Beef Franks, cut into 1-inch pieces

Preheat oven to 350°F. Heat oil in large saucepan over medium heat; add onion and garlic and cook 8 minutes, stirring occasionally. Add red and green bell peppers; cook 5 minutes, stirring occasionally. Stir in baked beans, butter beans, red beans, brown sugar, ketchup, vinegar and mustard; bring to a boil. Stir franks into bean mixture.

Transfer mixture to 2-quart casserole or 8- or 9-inch square baking dish. Bake 40 to 45 minutes or until hot and bubbly.   *Makes 6 main-dish or 10 side-dish servings*

Three Bean and Franks Bake

Patchwork Casserole

2 pounds ground beef

2 cups chopped green bell pepper

1 cup chopped onion

2 pounds frozen Southern-style hash-brown potatoes, thawed

2 cans (8 ounces each) tomato sauce

1 cup water

1 can (6 ounces) tomato paste

1 teaspoon salt

$^1/_2$ teaspoon dried basil leaves

$^1/_4$ teaspoon black pepper

1 pound pasteurized process American cheese, thinly sliced and divided

1. Preheat oven to 350°F.

2. Brown beef in large skillet over medium heat about 10 minutes; drain off fat. Add bell pepper and onion; cook and stir until tender, about 4 minutes. Stir in potatoes, tomato sauce, water, tomato paste, salt, basil and black pepper.

3. Spoon half of mixture into 13×9×2-inch baking pan or 3-quart baking dish; top with half of cheese. Spoon remaining beef mixture evenly on top of cheese. Cover pan with aluminum foil. Bake 45 minutes.

4. Cut remaining cheese into decorative shapes; place on top of casserole. Let stand loosely covered until cheese melts, about 5 minutes.   *Makes 8 to 10 servings*

Patchwork Casserole

Potato Sausage Casserole

1 pound bulk pork sausage or ground pork

1 can (10 ¾ ounces) condensed cream of mushroom soup, undiluted

¾ cup milk

½ cup chopped onion

½ teaspoon salt

¼ teaspoon black pepper

3 cups sliced potatoes

½ tablespoon butter, cut into small pieces

1 ½ cups (6 ounces) shredded Cheddar cheese

1. Preheat oven to 350°F. Spray 1 ½-quart casserole with nonstick cooking spray; set aside.

2. Cook sausage in large skillet over medium-high heat, stirring to separate, until no longer pink; drain fat.

3. Stir together soup, milk, onion, salt and pepper in medium bowl.

4. Place half of potatoes in prepared casserole. Top with half of soup mixture; top with half of sausage. Repeat layers, ending with sausage. Dot with butter.

5. Cover casserole with foil. Bake 1 ¼ to 1 ½ hours or until potatoes are tender. Uncover; sprinkle with cheese. Return to oven; bake until cheese is melted and casserole is bubbly.   *Makes 6 servings*

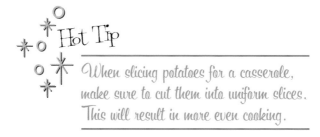

Hot Tip

When slicing potatoes for a casserole, make sure to cut them into uniform slices. This will result in more even cooking.

Chop Suey Casserole

2 cups (12 ounces) cooked roast beef strips

1 can (10¾ ounces) condensed cream of mushroom soup, undiluted

½ cup milk

1 package (10 ounces) frozen French-style green beans, thawed and drained

1 can (8 ounces) sliced water chestnuts, drained

½ cup diagonally sliced celery

2 tablespoons soy sauce

1⅓ cups *French's®* French Fried Onions, divided

1 medium tomato, cut into wedges

Preheat oven to 350°F. In large bowl, combine beef, soup, milk, beans, water chestnuts, celery, soy sauce and ⅔ *cup* French Fried Onions. Spoon beef mixture into 1½-quart casserole. Bake, covered, at 350°F for 30 minutes or until heated through. Arrange tomato wedges around edge of casserole and top with remaining ⅔ *cup* onions. Bake, uncovered, 5 minutes or until onions are golden brown.

Makes 4 servings

Microwave Directions: Prepare beef mixture as above; spoon into 1½-quart microwave-safe casserole. Cook, covered, on HIGH 10 to 12 minutes or until heated through. Stir beef mixture halfway through cooking time. Top with tomato wedges and remaining onions as above; cook, uncovered, 1 minute. Let stand 5 minutes.

Biscuit-Topped Hearty Steak Pie

1 1/2 pounds top round steak, cooked and cut into 1-inch cubes
1 package (9 ounces) frozen baby carrots
1 package (9 ounces) frozen peas and pearl onions
1 large baking potato, baked and cut into 1/2-inch pieces
1 jar (18 ounces) home-style brown gravy
1/2 teaspoon dried thyme leaves
1/2 teaspoon black pepper
1 can (10 ounces) refrigerated flaky buttermilk biscuits

✦ Preheat oven to 375°F. Spray 2-quart casserole with nonstick cooking spray.

✦ Combine steak, frozen vegetables and potato in prepared dish. Stir in gravy, thyme and pepper.

✦ Bake, uncovered, 40 minutes. Remove from oven. *Increase oven temperature to 400°F.* Top with biscuits and bake 8 to 10 minutes or until biscuits are golden brown.

Makes 6 servings

Hint: This casserole can be prepared with leftovers of almost any kind. Other steaks, roast beef, stew meat, pork, lamb or chicken can be substituted for the round steak; adjust the gravy flavor to complement the meat. Red potatoes can be used in place of the baking potato. Choose your favorite vegetable combination, such as broccoli, cauliflower and carrots, or broccoli, corn and red peppers, as a substitute for the peas and carrots.

Biscuit-Topped Hearty Steak Pie

Pork with Savory Apple Stuffing

1 package (6 ounces) corn bread stuffing mix
1 can (14½ ounces) chicken broth
1 small apple, peeled, cored and chopped
¼ cup chopped celery
1⅓ cups *French's®* French Fried Onions, divided
4 boneless pork chops, ¾ inch thick (about 1 pound)
½ cup peach-apricot sweet & sour sauce
1 tablespoon *French's®* Honey Dijon Mustard

1. Preheat oven to 375°F. Combine stuffing mix, broth, apple, celery and ⅔ cup French Fried Onions in large bowl. Spoon into bottom of greased shallow 2-quart baking dish. Arrange chops on top of stuffing.

2. Combine sweet & sour sauce with mustard in small bowl. Pour over pork. Bake 40 minutes or until pork is no longer pink in center.

3. Sprinkle with remaining onions. Bake 5 minutes or until onions are golden brown.

Makes 4 servings

Prep Time: 10 minutes ✦ Cook Time: 45 minutes

Hot Tip

To measure a round or oval casserole, fill a measuring cup with water and pour it into the empty dish. Repeat until it is filled with water, keeping track of the amount of water added. The amount of water is equivalent to the size of the dish.

66

Pork with Savory Apple Stuffing

Main-Dish Pie

1 package (8 rolls) refrigerated crescent rolls
1 pound lean ground beef
1 medium onion, chopped
1 can (12 ounces) beef or mushroom gravy
1 box (10 ounces) BIRDS EYE® frozen Green Peas, thawed
1/2 cup shredded Swiss cheese
6 slices tomato

✦ Unroll crescent dough and separate rolls. Spread to cover bottom of ungreased 9-inch pie pan. Press together to form crust. Bake in preheated 350°F oven for 10 minutes.

✦ In large skillet, brown ground beef and onion; drain excess fat.

✦ Stir in gravy and peas; cook until heated through.

✦ Pour mixture into partially baked crust. Sprinkle with cheese.

✦ Bake 10 to 15 minutes or until crust is brown and cheese is melted.

✦ Arrange tomato slices over pie; bake 2 minutes more.   *Makes 6 servings*

Prep Time: 10 minutes ✦ Cook Time: 22 to 27 minutes

68

Main-Dish Pie

Ham and Potato au Gratin

3 tablespoons butter or margarine

3 tablespoons all-purpose flour

2 cups milk

1 ½ cups (6 ounces) shredded Cheddar cheese

1 tablespoon Dijon mustard

2 cups HILLSHIRE FARM® Ham, cut into thin strips

1 package (24 ounces) frozen shredded hash brown potatoes, thawed

1 package (10 ounces) frozen chopped spinach, thawed and drained

Preheat oven to 350°F.

Melt butter in large saucepan over medium heat; stir in flour. Add milk. Cook and stir until bubbly; cook 1 minute more. Remove from heat. Stir in cheese and mustard; set aside.

Place ½ of Ham in ungreased medium casserole. Top with ½ of potatoes and ½ of milk mixture. Spoon spinach over top. Repeat layers with remaining ham, potatoes and milk mixture.

Bake, uncovered, 30 minutes or until heated through.   *Makes 8 servings*

Ham and Potato au Gratin

Tamale Pie

1 pound ground beef
1 package (10 ounces) frozen corn, thawed
1 can (14½ ounces) diced tomatoes, undrained
1 can (4 ounces) sliced black olives, drained
1 package (1¼ ounces) taco seasoning mix
1 package (6 ounces) corn muffin or corn bread mix plus ingredients to prepare mix
¼ cup (1 ounce) shredded Cheddar cheese
1 green onion, thinly sliced

1. Preheat oven to 400°F. Place beef in large skillet; cook over high heat 6 to 8 minutes or until no longer pink, stirring to separate. Pour off drippings. Add corn, tomatoes with juice, olives and seasoning mix to beef. Bring to a boil over medium-high heat, stirring constantly. Pour into deep 9-inch pie plate; smooth top with spatula.

2. Prepare corn muffin mix according to package directions. Spread evenly over beef mixture. Bake 8 to 10 minutes or until golden brown. Sprinkle with cheese and onion. Let stand 10 minutes before serving. Garnish as desired.   *Makes 6 servings*

Hot Tip

Store green onions in the refrigerator in a plastic bag for up to five days. Just before using, wash them thoroughly and trim off the roots. Next, remove any wilted or discolored layers. The onions can then be sliced, chopped, cut into lengths or used whole.

72

Tamale Pie

Countdown Casserole

1 jar (8 ounces) pasteurized process cheese spread
¾ cup milk
2 cups (12 ounces) cubed cooked roast beef
1 bag (16 ounces) frozen vegetable combination (broccoli, corn, red bell pepper), thawed and drained
4 cups frozen hash brown potatoes, thawed
1 ⅓ cups *French's*® French Fried Onions, divided
½ teaspoon seasoned salt
¼ teaspoon freshly ground black pepper
½ cup (2 ounces) shredded Cheddar cheese

Preheat oven to 375°F. Spoon cheese spread into 12×8-inch baking dish; place in oven just until cheese melts, about 5 minutes. Using fork, stir milk into melted cheese until well blended. Stir in beef, vegetables, potatoes, ⅔ cup French Fried Onions and the seasonings. Bake, covered, at 375°F 30 minutes or until heated through. Top with Cheddar cheese; sprinkle remaining ⅔ *cup* onions down center. Bake, uncovered, 3 minutes or until onions are golden brown.   *Makes 4 to 6 servings*

Microwave Directions: In 12×8-inch microwave-safe dish, combine cheese spread and milk. Cook, covered, on HIGH 3 minutes; stir. Add ingredients as directed. Cook, covered, 14 minutes or until heated through, stirring beef mixture halfway through cooking time. Top with Cheddar cheese and remaining ⅔ cup onions as directed. Cook, uncovered, 1 minute or until cheese melts. Let stand 5 minutes.

74

Countdown Casserole

Shepherd's Pie

1 1/3 cups instant mashed potato buds (4 servings)

1 2/3 cups milk

2 tablespoons margarine or butter

1 teaspoon salt, divided

1 pound ground beef

1/4 teaspoon black pepper

1 jar (12 ounces) beef gravy

1 package (10 ounces) frozen mixed vegetables, thawed and drained

3/4 cup grated Parmesan cheese

1. Preheat broiler. Prepare potatoes according to package directions using milk, margarine and 1/2 teaspoon salt.

2. While potatoes are cooking, brown beef in medium broilerproof skillet over medium-high heat, stirring to separate. Drain drippings. Sprinkle beef with remaining 1/2 teaspoon salt and pepper. Add gravy and vegetables; mix well. Cook over medium-low heat 5 minutes or until hot.

3. Spoon prepared potatoes around outside edge of skillet, leaving 3-inch circle in center. Sprinkle cheese evenly over potatoes. Broil 4 to 5 inches from heat 3 minutes or until cheese is golden brown and beef mixture is bubbly.   *Makes 4 servings*

Prep and Cook Time: 28 minutes

Shepherd's Pie

Biscuit-Topped Tuna Bake

 2 tablespoons vegetable oil

$1/2$ cup chopped onion

$1/2$ cup chopped celery

 1 can (10$3/4$ ounces) condensed cream of potato soup, undiluted

 1 package (10 ounces) frozen peas and carrots, thawed

 1 (7-ounce) pouch of STARKIST Flavor Fresh Pouch® Albacore or Chunk Light Tuna

$3/4$ cup milk

$1/4$ teaspoon ground black pepper

$1/4$ teaspoon garlic powder

 1 can (7$1/2$ ounces) refrigerator flaky biscuits

In large skillet, heat oil over medium-high heat; sauté onion and celery until onion is soft. Add remaining ingredients except biscuits; heat thoroughly. Transfer mixture to 1 $1/2$-quart casserole. Arrange biscuits around top edge of dish; bake in 400°F oven 10 to 15 minutes or until biscuits are golden brown.

Makes 4 to 6 servings

Prep and Cook Time: 25 minutes

Biscuit-Topped Tuna Bake

Baked Fish
with Potatoes and Onions

1 pound baking potatoes, very thinly sliced

1 large onion, very thinly sliced

1 small red or green bell pepper, thinly sliced

   Salt and black pepper

$1/2$ teaspoon dried oregano leaves

1 pound lean fish fillets, cut 1 inch thick

$1/4$ cup ($1/2$ stick) butter

$1/4$ cup all-purpose flour

2 cups milk

$3/4$ cup (3 ounces) shredded Cheddar cheese

✦ Preheat oven to 375°F.

✦ Arrange half of potatoes in buttered 3-quart casserole. Top with half of onion and half of bell pepper. Season with salt and black pepper. Sprinkle with half of oregano. Arrange fish in one layer over vegetables. Arrange remaining potatoes, onion and bell pepper over fish. Season with salt, black pepper and remaining oregano.

✦ Melt butter in medium saucepan over medium heat. Add flour; cook until bubbly, stirring constantly. Gradually stir in milk. Cook until thickened, stirring constantly. Pour white sauce over casserole. Cover; bake 40 minutes or until potatoes are tender. Sprinkle with cheese. Bake, uncovered, about 5 minutes or until cheese is melted.

Makes 4 servings

Baked Fish with Potatoes and Onions

Chesapeake Crab Strata

¼ cup (½ stick) butter

4 cups unseasoned croutons

2 cups (8 ounces) shredded Cheddar cheese

2 cups milk

8 eggs, beaten

½ teaspoon dry mustard

½ teaspoon seafood seasoning

   Salt and black pepper to taste

1 pound crabmeat, picked over to remove any shells

1. Preheat oven to 325°F. Place butter in 11×7-inch baking dish. Heat in oven until melted, tilting to coat dish. Remove dish from oven; spread croutons over melted butter. Top with cheese; set aside.

2. Combine milk, eggs, mustard, seafood seasoning, salt and black pepper; mix well. Pour egg mixture over cheese in dish; sprinkle with crabmeat. Bake 50 minutes or until mixture is set. Remove from oven and let stand about 10 minutes. Garnish as desired.   *Makes 6 to 8 servings*

82

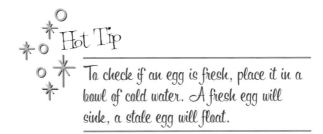

Hot Tip

To check if an egg is fresh, place it in a bowl of cold water. A fresh egg will sink, a stale egg will float.

Chesapeake Crab Strata

No-Fuss Tuna Quiche

1 unbaked 9-inch deep-dish pastry shell

1 1/2 cups low-fat milk

3 extra-large eggs

1/3 cup chopped green onions

1 tablespoon chopped drained pimiento

1 teaspoon dried basil leaves, crushed

1/2 teaspoon salt

1 (3-ounce) pouch of STARKIST Flavor Fresh Pouch® Albacore or Chunk Light Tuna

1/2 cup (2 ounces) shredded low-fat Cheddar cheese

8 spears (4 inches each) broccoli

Preheat oven to 450°F. Bake pastry shell for 5 minutes; remove to rack to cool. *Reduce oven temperature to 325°F.* For filling, in large bowl whisk together milk and eggs. Stir in onions, pimiento, basil and salt. Fold in tuna and cheese. Pour into prebaked pastry shell. Bake at 325°F for 30 minutes.

Meanwhile, in saucepan, steam broccoli spears over simmering water for 5 minutes. Drain; set aside. After 30 minutes baking time, arrange broccoli spears, spoke-fashion, over quiche. Bake 25 to 35 minutes more or until knife inserted 2 inches from center comes out clean. Let stand for 5 minutes. Cut into 8 wedges, centering broccoli spear in each wedge. *Makes 8 servings*

Note: If desired, 1 cup chopped broccoli can be added to the filling before baking.

84

No-Fuss Tuna Quiche

Creamy Shrimp & Vegetable Casserole

1 can (10³/₄ ounces) reduced-fat condensed cream of celery soup, undiluted

1 pound fresh or thawed frozen shrimp, shelled and deveined

¹/₂ cup sliced fresh or thawed frozen asparagus (1-inch pieces)

¹/₂ cup sliced mushrooms

¹/₄ cup sliced green onions

¹/₄ cup diced red bell pepper

1 clove garlic, minced

³/₄ teaspoon dried thyme leaves

¹/₄ teaspoon black pepper

   Hot cooked rice or orzo (optional)

1. Preheat oven to 375°F. Coat 2-quart baking dish with nonstick cooking spray.

2. Combine soup, shrimp, asparagus, mushrooms, green onions, bell pepper, garlic, thyme and black pepper in large bowl; mix well. Place in prepared baking dish.

3. Cover and bake 30 minutes. Serve over rice, if desired.   *Makes 4 servings*

86

Creamy Shrimp & Vegetable Casserole

Homestyle Tuna Pot Pie

- 1 package (15 ounces) refrigerated pie crust dough
- 1 can (10¾ ounces) condensed cream of potato or cream of mushroom soup, undiluted
- 1 package (10 ounces) frozen peas and carrots, thawed and drained
- 1 (7-ounce) pouch of STARKIST Flavor Fresh Pouch® Albacore or Chunk Light Tuna
- ½ cup chopped onion
- ⅓ cup milk
- ½ teaspoon poultry seasoning or dried thyme leaves
  - Salt and black pepper to taste

Line 9-inch pie pan with 1 pie crust dough round; set aside. Reserve second dough round. In medium bowl, combine remaining ingredients; mix well. Pour tuna mixture into pie shell; top with second crust. Crimp edges to seal. Cut slits in top crust to vent. Bake in 375°F oven 45 to 50 minutes or until golden brown.

Makes 6 servings

88

Prep and Cook Time: 55 to 60 minutes

Hot Tip

When making pies and quiches, it's important to choose the right pie plate. Heat-resistant glass or dull-finished metal pie plates provide the best browning. A shiny pan reflects heat, so the bottom crust can turn out underbaked and soggy.

Homestyle Tuna Pot Pie

Tuna and Broccoli Bake

1 package (16 ounces) frozen broccoli cuts, thawed and well drained

2 slices bread, cut in 1/2-inch cubes

1 (7-ounce) pouch of STARKIST Flavor Fresh Pouch® Albacore or Chunk Light Tuna

2 cups cottage cheese

1 cup shredded Cheddar cheese

3 eggs

1/4 teaspoon ground black pepper

Place broccoli on bottom of 2-quart baking dish. Top with bread cubes and tuna. In medium bowl, combine cottage cheese, Cheddar cheese, eggs and pepper. Spread evenly over tuna mixture. Bake in 400°F oven 30 minutes or until golden brown and puffed.   *Makes 4 servings*

Prep Time: 35 minutes

So-Easy Fish Divan

1 package (about 1 1/8 ounces) cheese sauce mix

1 1/3 cups milk

1 bag (16 ounces) frozen vegetable combination (brussels sprouts, carrots, cauliflower), thawed and drained

1 1/3 cups *French's®* French Fried Onions, divided

1 pound unbreaded fish fillets, thawed if frozen

1/2 cup (2 ounces) shredded Cheddar cheese

Preheat oven to 375°F. In small saucepan, prepare cheese sauce mix according to package directions using 1 1/3 cups milk. In 12×8-inch baking dish, combine vegetables and 2/3 *cup* French Fried Onions; top with fish fillets. Pour cheese sauce over fish and vegetables. Bake, covered, 25 minutes or until fish flakes easily with fork. Top fish with Cheddar cheese and remaining 2/3 *cup* onions; bake, uncovered, 3 minutes or until onions are golden brown.   *Makes 3 to 4 servings*

Tuna and Broccoli Bake

Impossibly Easy Salmon Pie

1 can (7 ½ ounces) salmon packed in water, drained and deboned
½ cup grated Parmesan cheese
¼ cup sliced green onions
1 jar (2 ounces) chopped pimientos, drained
½ cup low-fat (1%) cottage cheese
1 tablespoon lemon juice
1 ½ cups low-fat (1%) milk
¾ cup reduced-fat baking mix
2 whole eggs
2 egg whites *or* ¼ cup cholesterol-free egg substitute
¼ teaspoon salt
¼ teaspoon dried dill weed
¼ teaspoon paprika (optional)

1. Preheat oven to 375°F. Spray 9-inch pie plate with nonstick cooking spray. Combine salmon, Parmesan cheese, onions and pimientos in prepared pie plate; set aside.

2. Combine cottage cheese and lemon juice in blender or food processor; blend until smooth. Add milk, baking mix, whole eggs, egg whites, salt and dill. Blend 15 seconds. Pour over salmon mixture in pie plate. Sprinkle with paprika, if desired.

3. Bake 35 to 40 minutes or until lightly golden and knife inserted halfway between center and edge comes out clean. Cool 5 minutes. Garnish as desired. Cut into 8 wedges.

Makes 8 servings

Impossibly Easy Salmon Pie

Scallop and Artichoke Heart Casserole

    1 package (9 ounces) frozen artichoke hearts, cooked and drained
    1 pound scallops
    1 teaspoon canola or vegetable oil
    ¼ cup chopped red bell pepper
    ¼ cup sliced green onion tops
    ¼ cup all-purpose flour
    2 cups low-fat (1%) milk
    1 teaspoon dried tarragon leaves, crushed
    ¼ teaspoon salt
    ¼ teaspoon white pepper
    1 tablespoon chopped fresh parsley
      Dash paprika

✦ Cut large artichoke hearts lengthwise into halves. Arrange artichoke hearts in even layer in 8-inch square baking dish.

✦ Rinse scallops; pat dry with paper towel. If scallops are large, cut into halves. Arrange scallops evenly over artichokes.

✦ Preheat oven to 350°F. Heat oil in medium saucepan over medium-low heat. Add bell pepper and green onions; cook and stir 5 minutes or until tender. Stir in flour. Gradually stir in milk until smooth. Add tarragon, salt and white pepper; cook and stir over medium heat 10 minutes or until sauce boils and thickens.

✦ Pour hot sauce over scallops. Bake, uncovered, 25 minutes or until bubbling and scallops are opaque. Sprinkle with chopped parsley and paprika before serving.

Makes 4 servings

Tag-Along Tuna Bake

3 to 4 tablespoons butter or margarine, softened

12 slices bread

1 can (12 $\frac{1}{2}$ ounces) water-packed tuna, drained and flaked

1 cup chopped celery

1 $\frac{1}{3}$ cups *French's*® French Fried Onions, divided

2 cups milk

1 can (10$\frac{3}{4}$ ounces) condensed cream of mushroom soup, undiluted

1 cup mayonnaise

4 eggs, lightly beaten

3 slices ($\frac{3}{4}$ ounce each) processed American cheese, cut diagonally into halves

Butter 1 side of each bread slice; arrange 6 slices, buttered-side down in 13×9-inch baking dish. Layer tuna, celery and ⅔ cup French Fried Onions evenly over bread. Top with remaining bread slices, buttered side down. In medium bowl, combine milk, soup, mayonnaise and eggs; mix well. Pour evenly over layers in baking dish; cover and refrigerate overnight. Bake, covered, at 350°F for 30 minutes. Uncover and bake 15 minutes or until center is set. Arrange cheese slices down center of casserole, overlapping slightly, points all in one direction. Top with remaining ⅔ cup onions; bake, uncovered, 5 minutes or until onions are golden brown.   *Makes 8 servings*

95

Easy Three Cheese Tuna Soufflé

4 cups large croutons*

2 1/2 cups milk

1 can (10 3/4 ounces) condensed cream of celery soup, undiluted

4 large eggs

3 cups shredded cheese, use a combination of Cheddar, Monterey Jack and Swiss

1 (7-ounce) pouch of STARKIST Flavor Fresh Pouch® Albacore or Chunk Light Tuna

1 tablespoon butter or margarine

1/2 cup chopped celery

1/2 cup finely chopped onion

1/4 pound mushrooms, sliced

Use garlic and herb or ranch-flavored croutons.

In bottom of lightly greased 13×9-inch baking dish, arrange croutons. In medium bowl, beat together milk, soup and eggs; stir in cheeses and tuna. In small skillet, melt butter over medium heat. Add celery, onion and mushrooms; sauté until onion is soft.

Spoon sautéed vegetables over croutons; pour egg-tuna mixture over top. Cover; refrigerate overnight. Remove from refrigerator 1 hour before baking; bake in 325°F oven 45 to 50 minutes or until hot and bubbly.   *Makes 8 servings*

Prep and Cook Time: 60 minutes

Easy Three Cheese Tuna Soufflé

Shrimp Primavera Pot Pie

1 can (10 3/4 ounces) condensed cream of shrimp soup, undiluted
1 package (12 ounces) frozen peeled uncooked medium shrimp
2 packages (1 pound each) frozen mixed vegetables, such as green beans, potatoes, onions and red peppers, thawed and drained
1 teaspoon dried dill weed
1/4 teaspoon *each* salt and black pepper
1 can (11 ounces) refrigerated breadstick dough, separated into 8 strips

Preheat oven to 400°F. For filling, heat soup in ovenproof skillet over medium-high heat 1 minute. Add shrimp; cook and stir 3 minutes or until shrimp begin to thaw. Stir in vegetables and seasonings. Reduce heat to medium-low; cook and stir 3 minutes. Twist dough strips; arrange over filling, securing ends to skillet. Bake 18 minutes or until crust is golden and filling is bubbly.   *Makes 4 to 6 servings*

Fillets Stuffed with Crabmeat

1 envelope **LIPTON® RECIPE SECRETS®** Savory Herb with Garlic Soup Mix*
1/2 cup fresh bread crumbs
1 package (6 ounces) frozen crabmeat, thawed and well drained
1/2 cup water
2 teaspoons lemon juice
4 fish fillets (about 1 pound)
1 tablespoon **I CAN'T BELIEVE IT'S NOT BUTTER!®** Spread, melted

*Also terrific with LIPTON® RECIPE SECRETS® Golden Onion Soup Mix.

Preheat oven to 350°F.

In medium bowl, combine soup mix, bread crumbs, crabmeat, water and lemon juice.

Top fillets evenly with crabmeat mixture; roll up and secure with wooden toothpicks. Place in lightly greased 2-quart oblong baking dish. Brush fish with I Can't Believe It's Not Butter!® Spread and bake 25 minutes or until fish flakes. Remove toothpicks before serving.   *Makes 4 servings*

Shrimp Primavera Pot Pie

Fish Broccoli Casserole

1 package (10 ounces) frozen broccoli spears, thawed, drained
1 cup cooked flaked Florida whitefish
1 can (10¾ ounces) condensed cream of mushroom soup, undiluted
½ cup milk
¼ teaspoon salt
⅛ teaspoon freshly ground black pepper
½ cup crushed potato chips

Preheat oven to 425°F. Grease 1 ½-quart casserole. Layer broccoli in prepared casserole. Combine fish, soup, milk, salt and pepper in large bowl.

Spread fish mixture over broccoli. Sprinkle with potato chips. Bake 12 to 15 minutes or until golden brown.   *Makes 4 servings*

Favorite recipe from **Florida Department of Agriculture and Consumer Services, Bureau of Seafood and Aquaculture**

Hot Tip

Whitefish is a member of the salmon family. It has firm, white flesh and a mild flavor. Fresh whitefish is generally available in fillets or whole. Whitefish fillets are also readily available frozen.

Fish Broccoli Casserole

Sausage and Broccoli Noodle Casserole

1 jar (1 pound) RAGÚ® Cheese Creations!® Classic Alfredo Sauce
1/3 cup milk
1 pound sweet Italian sausage, cooked and crumbled
1 package (9 ounces) frozen chopped broccoli, thawed
8 ounces egg noodles, cooked and drained
1 cup shredded Cheddar cheese (about 4 ounces), divided
1/4 cup chopped roasted red peppers

1. Preheat oven to 350°F. In large bowl, combine Ragú Cheese Creations! Sauce and milk. Stir in sausage, broccoli, noodles, 3/4 cup cheese and roasted peppers.

2. In 13×9-inch baking dish, evenly spread sausage mixture. Sprinkle with remaining 1/4 cup cheese.

3. Bake 30 minutes or until heated through.

Makes 6 servings

Prep Time: 15 minutes ✦ Cook Time: 30 minutes

Hint: Substitute sausage with equal amounts of vegetables for a hearty vegetarian entrée.

Sausage and Broccoli Noodle Casserole

String Pie

1 pound ground beef

1/2 cup chopped onion

1/4 cup chopped green bell pepper

1 jar (15 1/2 ounces) spaghetti sauce

8 ounces spaghetti, cooked and drained

1/3 cup grated Parmesan cheese

2 eggs, beaten

2 teaspoons butter, melted

1 cup cottage cheese

1/2 cup (2 ounces) shredded mozzarella cheese

Preheat oven to 350°F. Cook beef, onion and green pepper in large skillet over medium-high heat until meat is browned. Drain fat. Stir in spaghetti sauce. Combine spaghetti, Parmesan cheese, eggs and melted butter in large bowl; mix well. Place in 13×9-inch baking pan. Spread cottage cheese over top; cover with sauce mixture. Sprinkle with mozzarella cheese. Bake until mixture is thoroughly heated and cheese is melted, about 20 minutes.   *Makes 6 to 8 servings*

Favorite recipe from **North Dakota Beef Commission**

Hot Tip

Pasta is finished cooking when it is tender but still firm to the bite. The pasta continues to cook when the casserole is placed in the oven, so it is important that the pasta be slightly undercooked.

String Pie

Creamy Chicken and Pasta with Spinach

6 ounces uncooked egg noodles

1 tablespoon olive oil

¼ cup chopped onion

¼ cup chopped red bell pepper

1 package (10 ounces) frozen spinach, thawed and drained

2 boneless skinless chicken breasts (¾ pound), cooked and cut into 1-inch pieces

1 can (4 ounces) sliced mushrooms, drained

2 cups (8 ounces) shredded Swiss cheese

1 container (8 ounces) sour cream

¾ cup half-and-half

2 eggs, lightly beaten

½ teaspoon salt

Red onion and fresh spinach (optional)

1. Preheat oven to 350°F. Prepare noodles according to package directions; set aside. Spray 13×9-inch baking dish with nonstick cooking spray; set aside.

2. Heat oil in large skillet over medium-high heat. Add onion and bell pepper; cook and stir 2 minutes or until onion is tender. Add spinach, chicken, mushrooms and cooked noodles; stir to blend.

3. Combine cheese, sour cream, half-and-half, eggs and salt in medium bowl; blend well.

4. Add cheese mixture to chicken mixture; stir to blend. Transfer to prepared baking dish. Bake, covered, 30 to 35 minutes or until heated through. Garnish with red onion and fresh spinach, if desired.   *Makes 8 servings*

Creamy Chicken and Pasta with Spinach

Tomato Pesto Lasagna

8 ounces lasagna noodles (2 inches wide)

I pound crumbled sausage or ground beef

I can (14 1/2 ounces) DEL MONTE® Diced Tomatoes with Garlic & Onion

I can (6 ounces) DEL MONTE Tomato Paste

8 ounces ricotta cheese

I package (4 ounces) pesto sauce*

2 cups (8 ounces) shredded mozzarella cheese

Grated Parmesan cheese (optional)

Pesto sauce is available frozen or refrigerated at the supermarket.

1. Cook noodles according to package directions; rinse, drain and separate noodles.

2. Meanwhile, brown meat in large skillet; drain. Stir in undrained tomatoes, tomato paste and 3/4 cup water.

3. Layer 1/3 meat sauce, then half each of noodles, ricotta cheese, pesto and mozzarella cheese in 2-quart casserole or 9-inch square baking dish; repeat layers. Top with remaining meat sauce. Sprinkle with grated Parmesan cheese, if desired.

4. Bake at 350°F 30 minutes or until heated through. *Makes 6 servings*

Prep Time: 20 minutes ✦ Cook Time: 30 minutes

Microwave Directions: Assemble lasagna in 9-inch square microwavable dish as directed. Cover with vented plastic wrap; microwave on HIGH 10 minutes, rotating dish after 5 minutes.

Tomato Pesto Lasagna

Meatball Stroganoff

1 can (10¾ ounces) condensed cream of mushroom soup, undiluted

1 container (8 ounces) sour cream

1 cup milk

1 package (15 ounces) frozen prepared meatballs, thawed and cut in half if large

4 cups cooked egg noodles (5 ounces uncooked)

1 cup (4 ounces) shredded Swiss cheese

2 cups *French's*® French Fried Onions, divided

¼ cup minced fresh parsley

1 tablespoon *French's*® Worcestershire Sauce

1 teaspoon paprika

1. Preheat oven to 350°F. Coat 3-quart shallow baking dish with vegetable cooking spray.

2. Combine soup, sour cream and milk in large bowl. Stir in meatballs, noodles, cheese, *1 cup* French Fried Onions, parsley, Worcestershire and paprika. Spoon into prepared baking dish.

3. Bake 25 minutes or until heated through. Stir. Sprinkle with remaining *1 cup* onions; bake 5 minutes or until onions are golden brown.   *Makes 4 servings*

Prep Time: 10 minutes ✦ Cook Time: 30 minutes

Quick Turkey Tetrazzini

1/2 cup chopped onion

2 tablespoons butter or margarine

1 (10 3/4-ounce) can condensed cream of mushroom soup, undiluted

3/4 cup water

1/2 cup shredded Cheddar cheese

2 (5-ounce) cans HORMEL® chunk turkey, drained and flaked

2 tablespoons chopped fresh parsley

2 tablespoons chopped pimiento

1/4 teaspoon black pepper

4 cups cooked spaghetti

1/4 cup grated Parmesan cheese

Salt and black pepper

In large saucepan or Dutch oven, cook onion in butter until tender. Stir in soup; gradually stir in water. Add Cheddar cheese; heat, stirring frequently, until cheese melts. Remove from heat. Stir in turkey, parsley, pimiento, and pepper. Toss mixture with spaghetti; mix well. Pour into 2-quart casserole. Sprinkle Parmesan cheese over top. Bake in preheated 350°F oven 30 minutes or until hot and bubbly. Season to taste with salt and pepper.   *Makes 6 to 8 servings*

Make Ahead Directions: Prepare as directed, but do not bake. Cover; refrigerate several hours or overnight. Remove cover. Bake in preheated 350°F oven 35 to 40 minutes or until hot and bubbly.

111

Country Sausage
Macaroni and Cheese

  1 **pound BOB EVANS® Special Seasonings Roll Sausage**

1 ½ **cups milk**

12 **ounces pasteurized processed Cheddar cheese, cut into cubes**

  ½ **cup Dijon mustard**

  1 **cup diced fresh or drained canned tomatoes**

  1 **cup sliced mushrooms**

  ⅓ **cup sliced green onions**

  ⅛ **teaspoon cayenne pepper**

12 **ounces uncooked elbow macaroni**

  2 **tablespoons grated Parmesan cheese**

Preheat oven to 350°F. Crumble and cook sausage in medium skillet until browned. Drain on paper towels. Combine milk, processed cheese and mustard in medium saucepan; cook and stir over low heat until cheese melts and mixture is smooth. Stir in sausage, tomatoes, mushrooms, green onions and cayenne pepper. Remove from heat.

Cook macaroni according to package directions; drain. Combine hot macaroni and cheese mixture in large bowl; toss until well coated. Spoon into greased shallow 2-quart casserole dish. Cover and bake 15 to 20 minutes. Stir; sprinkle with Parmesan cheese. Bake, uncovered, 5 minutes more. Let stand 10 minutes before serving. Refrigerate leftovers.

Makes 6 to 8 servings

Country Sausage Macaroni and Cheese

Artichoke-Olive Chicken Bake

1 ½ cups uncooked rotini
1 tablespoon olive oil
1 medium onion, chopped
½ green bell pepper, chopped
2 cups shredded cooked chicken
1 can (14½ ounces) diced tomatoes with Italian-style herbs, undrained
1 can (14 ounces) artichoke hearts, drained and quartered
1 can (6 ounces) sliced black olives, drained
1 teaspoon dried Italian seasoning
2 cups (8 ounces) shredded mozzarella cheese

✦ Preheat oven to 350°F. Spray 2-quart casserole with nonstick cooking spray.

✦ Cook pasta according to package directions until al dente. Drain.

✦ Heat oil in large deep skillet over medium heat until hot. Add onion and pepper; cook and stir 1 minute. Add pasta, chicken, tomatoes with juice, artichokes, olives and Italian seasoning; mix until blended.

✦ Place half of chicken mixture in prepared dish; sprinkle with half of cheese. Top with remaining chicken mixture and cheese.

✦ Bake, covered, 35 minutes or until hot and bubbly.   *Makes 8 servings*

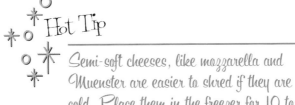

Hot Tip

Semi-soft cheeses, like mozzarella and Muenster are easier to shred if they are cold. Place them in the freezer for 10 to 15 minutes before shredding.

114

Artichoke-Olive Chicken Bake

Zesty Seafood Lasagna

2 packages (1.8 ounces each) white sauce mix

4 1/2 cups milk

1 teaspoon dried basil leaves

1/2 teaspoon dried thyme leaves

1/2 teaspoon garlic powder

3/4 cup grated Parmesan cheese, divided

3 tablespoons *Frank's*® *RedHot*® Original Cayenne Pepper Sauce

9 oven-ready lasagna pasta sheets

2 packages (10 ounces each) frozen chopped spinach, thawed and squeezed

1/2 pound cooked shrimp

1/2 pound raw bay scallops or flaked imitation crabmeat

2 cups (8 ounces) shredded mozzarella cheese, divided

1. Preheat oven to 400°F. Prepare white sauce according to package directions using milk and adding basil, thyme and garlic powder in large saucepan. Stir in 1/2 cup Parmesan cheese and *Frank's RedHot* Sauce.

2. Spread 1 cup sauce on bottom of greased 13×9×2-inch casserole. Layer 3 pasta sheets crosswise over sauce. (Do not let edges touch.) Layer half of the spinach and seafood over pasta. Spoon 1 cup sauce over seafood; sprinkle with 3/4 cup mozzarella cheese. Repeat layers a second time. Top with final layer of pasta sheets, remaining sauce and cheeses.

3. Cover pan with greased foil. Bake 40 minutes. Remove foil; bake 10 minutes or until top is browned and pasta is fully cooked. Let stand 15 minutes before serving.

Makes 8 servings

Prep Time: 30 minutes ✦ Cook Time: 50 minutes

Hint: Splash *Frank's RedHot* Sauce on foods after cooking instead of salt and black pepper. *Frank's RedHot* Sauce perks up the flavor of all foods!

Zesty Seafood Lasagna

Broccoli & Cheddar Noodle Casserole

1 package (12 ounces) dry wide egg noodles
3 tablespoons margarine or butter, divided
2 cups chopped onions
4 cups broccoli flowerets
1 can (14.5 ounces) CONTADINA® Stewed Tomatoes, undrained
1 can (6 ounces) CONTADINA Tomato Paste
1 package (1 1/2 ounces) spaghetti sauce seasoning mix
2 cups water
1 teaspoon garlic salt
1 1/2 cups (6 ounces) shredded Cheddar cheese
1/2 cup CONTADINA Seasoned Italian Bread Crumbs

118

1. Cook noodles according to package directions; drain.

2. Meanwhile, melt 2 tablespoons margarine in 5-quart saucepan; sauté onions until tender.

3. Stir in broccoli, undrained tomatoes, tomato paste, seasoning mix, water and garlic salt. Bring to a boil. Reduce heat; simmer, uncovered, for 10 minutes, stirring occasionally. Stir in cooked noodles.

4. Layer half of the noodle mixture in 13×9×2-inch baking dish. Sprinkle with cheese. Layer with remaining noodle mixture.

5. Melt remaining 1 tablespoon margarine; stir in crumbs. Sprinkle over casserole; cover and bake in preheated 350°F oven 20 minutes. Uncover; bake 5 minutes.

Makes 6 servings

Prep Time: 25 minutes ✦ Cook Time: 25 minutes

Broccoli & Cheddar Noodle Casserole

Polish Reuben Casserole

2 cans (10¾ ounces each) condensed cream of mushroom soup, undiluted

1 ⅓ cups milk

½ cup chopped onion

1 tablespoon prepared mustard

2 cans (16 ounces each) sauerkraut, rinsed and drained

1 package (8 ounces) uncooked medium-width noodles

1 ½ pounds Polish sausage, cut into ½-inch pieces

2 cups (8 ounces) shredded Swiss cheese

¾ cup whole wheat bread crumbs

2 tablespoons butter, melted

1. Preheat oven to 350°F. Grease 13×9-inch baking dish.

2. Combine soup, milk, onion and mustard in medium bowl; blend well. Spread sauerkraut in prepared dish. Top with uncooked noodles. Spoon soup mixture evenly over noodles; cover with sausage. Top with cheese. Combine bread crumbs and butter in small bowl; sprinkle over casserole.

3. Cover dish tightly with foil. Bake about 1 hour or until noodles are tender. Garnish as desired. *Makes 8 to 10 servings*

Polish Reuben Casserole

Tuna-Noodle Casserole

    1 tablespoon butter
³/₄ cup diced onion
    1 can (10³/₄ ounces) condensed cream of mushroom soup, undiluted
    1 cup milk
    3 cups hot cooked egg noodles
    2 cans (about 6 ounces each) tuna, drained and flaked
1 ¹/₄ cups frozen peas
    1 jar (2 ounces) diced pimientos, drained
    1 tablespoon lemon juice
¹/₄ teaspoon salt
¹/₄ teaspoon black pepper
¹/₂ cup fresh bread crumbs
¹/₂ cup grated **BELGIOIOSO®** Parmesan Cheese

Preheat oven to 450°F. Melt butter in medium saucepan over medium-high heat. Add onion; sauté 3 minutes. Add soup and milk. Cook 3 minutes, whisking constantly. Combine soup mixture, noodles, tuna, peas, pimientos, lemon juice, salt and pepper in 2-quart casserole. Combine bread crumbs and BelGioioso Parmesan Cheese in separate bowl; sprinkle over tuna mixture. Bake at 450°F for 15 minutes or until hot and bubbly.   *Makes 4 servings*

Chicken Lasagne Rolls

    8 uncooked lasagne noodles
    1 package (10 ounces) frozen chopped spinach, thawed
    2 cups chopped cooked chicken
 1 ½ cups lowfat cottage cheese
    3 sliced green onions
    2 tablespoons diced pimiento
  ½ teaspoon salt
  ¼ teaspoon black pepper
    1 jar (12 ounces) HEINZ® HomeStyle or Fat Free Classic Chicken Gravy
    1 can (4 ounces) sliced mushrooms, drained
    1 cup finely shredded Swiss or mozzarella cheese, divided
      Paprika

Cook lasagne noodles according to package directions; set aside. Squeeze spinach dry. In small bowl, combine spinach, chicken and next 5 ingredients. Spread about ½ cup spinach mixture on each noodle; roll up jelly-roll fashion. Place seam-side down in lightly greased 13×9-inch baking pan. Combine gravy, mushrooms and ½ cup Swiss cheese; pour over rolls. Cover; bake in preheated 350°F. oven 40 to 45 minutes. Sprinkle with remaining ½ cup Swiss cheese and paprika. Bake an additional 10 to 15 minutes or until cheese is melted and rolls are heated through.

Makes 4 to 6 servings

123

Hot Tip

Pasta should be cooked at a fast boil. The rolling motion of the water circulates the pasta during cooking so that it cooks more evenly.

Lemony Dill Salmon and Shell Casserole

Nonstick cooking spray
1 ½ cups sliced mushrooms
⅓ cup sliced green onions
1 clove garlic, minced
2 cups fat-free (skim) milk
3 tablespoons all-purpose flour
1 tablespoon grated lemon peel
¾ teaspoon dried dill weed
¼ teaspoon salt
⅛ teaspoon black pepper
1 ½ cups frozen green peas
1 can (7 ½ ounces) salmon, drained and flaked
6 ounces uncooked medium shell pasta, cooked, rinsed and drained

1. Preheat oven to 350°F.

2. Spray medium nonstick saucepan with cooking spray; heat over medium heat until hot. Add mushrooms, onions and garlic; cook and stir 5 minutes or until vegetables are tender.

3. Combine milk and flour in medium bowl until smooth. Stir in lemon peel, dill weed, salt and pepper. Cook over medium-high heat 5 to 8 minutes or until thickened, stirring constantly. Remove saucepan from heat. Stir in peas, salmon and pasta. Transfer pasta mixture to 2-quart casserole.

4. Bake, covered, 35 to 40 minutes. Garnish as desired. Serve immediately.

Makes 6 servings

Lemony Dill Salmon and Shell Casserole

Macaroni & Cheese with Bacon

3 cups (8 ounces) uncooked rotini pasta

2 tablespoons butter

2 tablespoons all-purpose flour

¼ teaspoon salt

¼ teaspoon dry mustard

⅛ teaspoon black pepper

1 ½ cups milk

2 cups (8 ounces) shredded sharp Cheddar cheese

8 ounces bacon, crisply cooked and crumbled*

2 medium tomatoes, sliced

* 1 cup cubed cooked ham can be substituted for bacon.

1. Preheat oven to 350°F. Lightly grease 1 ½-quart shallow casserole.

2. Cook pasta according to package directions; drain and return to saucepan.

3. Melt butter over medium-low heat in 2-quart saucepan. Whisk in flour, salt, mustard and pepper; cook and stir 1 minute. Whisk in milk. Bring to a boil over medium heat, stirring frequently. Reduce heat and simmer 2 minutes. Remove from heat. Add cheese; stir until melted.

4. Add cheese mixture and bacon to pasta; stir until well blended. Transfer to prepared casserole. Bake uncovered 20 minutes. Arrange tomato slices on casserole. Bake additional 5 to 8 minutes or until casserole is bubbly and tomatoes are hot.

Makes 4 servings

Macaroni & Cheese with Bacon

Seafood Newburg Casserole

1 can (10¾ ounces) condensed cream of shrimp soup, undiluted

½ cup half-and-half

1 tablespoon dry sherry

¼ teaspoon ground red pepper

3 cups cooked rice

2 cans (6 ounces each) lump crabmeat, drained

¼ pound raw medium shrimp, peeled and deveined

¼ pound raw bay scallops

1 jar (4 ounces) pimientos, drained and chopped

¼ cup finely chopped fresh parsley

✦ Preheat oven to 350°F. Spray 2½-quart casserole with nonstick cooking spray.

✦ Whisk together soup, half-and-half, sherry and red pepper in large bowl until blended. Add rice, crabmeat, shrimp, scallops and pimientos; toss well.

✦ Transfer mixture to prepared casserole; sprinkle with parsley. Cover; bake about 25 minutes or until shrimp and scallops are opaque.

Makes 6 servings

Seafood Newburg Casserole

Oven Chicken & Rice

1 can (10¾ ounces) condensed cream of mushroom soup, undiluted

1⅓ cups water

1 cup uncooked long-grain rice

1 teaspoon dried dill weed, divided

¼ teaspoon black pepper

1 chicken (3 pounds), cut up and skinned

½ cup crushed multi-grain crackers

1 teaspoon paprika

2 tablespoons butter, melted

Preheat oven to 375°F. Combine soup, water, rice, ¾ teaspoon dill and pepper in 13×9-inch baking dish; place chicken pieces on top. Cover with foil. Bake 45 minutes. Sprinkle chicken with crackers, paprika and remaining ¼ teaspoon dill. Drizzle with butter. Bake 5 to 10 minutes or until chicken is tender.   *Makes 4 to 5 servings*

Jackpot Casserole

2 tablespoons butter or olive oil

2 medium onions, chopped

2 ribs celery, chopped

1 can (4 ounces) sliced mushrooms, drained

1 to 1½ pounds ground beef

1 can (4 ounces) sliced olives, drained

1½ cups cooked rice

1 can (8 ounces) tomato sauce

Preheat oven to 350°F. Melt butter in skillet over medium heat. Add onions and celery; cook and stir until almost tender. Add mushrooms; cook and stir until all vegetables are tender. In another skillet, cook and stir beef over medium-high heat 10 minutes or until no longer pink; drain fat. Mix vegetables, beef, olives and rice in 3- to 4-quart casserole. Add sauce; mix well. Cover; bake 1 hour or until hot.   *Makes 4 to 6 servings*

Oven Chicken & Rice

Flounder Fillets over Zesty Lemon Rice

$\frac{1}{4}$ cup ($\frac{1}{2}$ stick) butter

3 tablespoons fresh lemon juice

2 teaspoons chicken bouillon granules

$\frac{1}{2}$ teaspoon black pepper

1 cup cooked rice

1 package (10 ounces) frozen chopped broccoli, thawed

1 cup (4 ounces) shredded sharp Cheddar cheese

1 pound flounder fillets

$\frac{1}{2}$ teaspoon paprika

1. Preheat oven to 375°F. Spray 2-quart casserole with nonstick cooking spray.

2. Melt butter in small saucepan over medium heat. Add lemon juice, bouillon granules and pepper; cook and stir 2 minutes or until bouillon granules dissolve.

3. Combine rice, broccoli, cheese and $\frac{1}{4}$ cup lemon sauce in medium bowl; spread on bottom of prepared dish. Place fillets over rice mixture. Pour remaining lemon sauce over fillets.

4. Bake, uncovered, 20 minutes or until fish flakes easily when tested with fork. Sprinkle evenly with paprika. *Makes 6 servings*

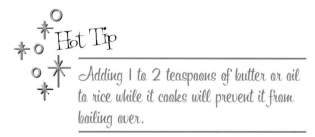

Hot Tip

Adding 1 to 2 teaspoons of butter or oil to rice while it cooks will prevent it from boiling over.

133

Flounder Fillets over Zesty Lemon Rice

Cheesy Tuna Pie

2 cups cooked rice

2 cans (**6** ounces each) tuna, drained and flaked

1 cup mayonnaise

1 cup (**4** ounces) shredded Cheddar cheese

1 can (**4** ounces) sliced black olives

½ cup thinly sliced celery

½ cup sour cream

2 tablespoons onion flakes

1 refrigerated pie crust dough

Preheat oven to 350°F. Spray 9-inch deep-dish pie pan with nonstick cooking spray. Combine all ingredients except pie crust in bowl; mix well. Spoon into prepared pie pan. Place pie crust over tuna mixture; press edge to pie pan to seal. Cut slits for steam. Bake 20 minutes or until crust is browned and filling is bubbly.   *Makes 6 servings*

134

Wild Rice and Turkey Casserole

1 can (**10¾** ounces) low-fat condensed cream of celery soup, undiluted

2½ cups water

1 cup uncooked wild rice mixture

1 tablespoon **MRS. DASH**® Onion & Herb Blend

¼ pound cooked turkey, shredded

Vegetable cooking spray

Preheat oven to 375°F. Spray a 2-quart casserole with vegetable cooking spray. Place soup in casserole. Stir water slowly into the soup. Add rice, Onion & Herb Blend and turkey; mix well. Bake, uncovered, 45 minutes. Remove from the oven and stir again. Return to the oven and bake an additional 15 minutes. Let stand for 5 minutes before serving.   *Makes 6 servings*

Prep Time: 5 minutes ✦ **Cook Time:** 60 minutes

135

Cheesy Tuna Pie

City Chicken BBQ Casserole

2 tablespoons vegetable oil

6 to 8 boneless pork chops (about 2 pounds), cut into bite-size pieces

1/4 cup chopped onions

2 cloves garlic, chopped

2 cups water

2 cups uncooked instant white rice

2 cups (8 ounces) shredded mozzarella cheese

Sauce

1 bottle (12 ounces) chili sauce

1 cup ketchup

1/2 cup packed brown sugar

2 tablespoons honey

1 tablespoon *each* Worcestershire sauce and hot pepper jelly

1 teaspoon *each* ground ginger and liquid smoke

1/2 teaspoon curry powder

1/4 teaspoon black pepper

1. Preheat oven to 350°F.

2. Heat oil in large skillet over medium-high heat until hot. Add pork; cook and stir 10 to 15 minutes or until browned and barely pink in center. Add onions and garlic; cook until onions are tender. Drain fat.

3. Meanwhile, bring water to a boil in small saucepan. Stir in rice; cover. Remove from heat; let stand 5 minutes or until water is absorbed.

4. Combine all sauce ingredients in separate saucepan; bring to a boil. Reduce heat to low; cover and simmer 10 minutes, stirring occasionally.

5. Combine pork mixture, rice and sauce in 2 1/2-quart casserole; mix well. Bake 15 to 20 minutes. Top with mozzarella cheese; bake 5 minutes. Serve hot.

Makes 6 to 8 servings

Note: "City chicken" is a traditional dish in Ohio and Pennsylvania. The name indicates that chicken was once more expensive than pork, so the cheaper pork cuts were prepared to taste like chicken.

City Chicken BBQ Casserole

Meat Crust Pie

1 pound 90% lean ground beef

2 cans (8 ounces each) tomato sauce, divided

1/2 cup seasoned dry bread crumbs

1/2 cup chopped green bell pepper, divided

1/4 cup minced onion

1 teaspoon salt, divided

1/8 teaspoon dried oregano leaves

1/8 teaspoon black pepper

1 cup water

1 1/3 cups instant rice

1 cup (4 ounces) shredded Cheddar cheese, divided

1. Preheat oven to 350°F. Combine beef, 1/2 cup tomato sauce, bread crumbs, 1/4 cup bell pepper, onion, 1/2 teaspoon salt, oregano and pepper in large bowl; mix well. Pat onto bottom and up side of ungreased 9-inch deep-dish pie plate.

2. Bring water and remaining 1/2 teaspoon salt to a boil in medium saucepan. Stir in rice; cover and remove from heat. Let stand 5 minutes or until water is absorbed. Add remaining 1 1/2 cups tomato sauce, 1/2 cup cheese and remaining 1/4 cup bell pepper to rice; mix well. Spoon rice mixture into meat shell. Cover with foil; bake 25 minutes.

3. Remove from oven and drain fat carefully, holding pan lid over pie to keep it from sliding. Top with remaining 1/2 cup cheese. Bake, uncovered, 10 to 15 minutes or until cheese melts. Carefully drain fat again. Garnish as desired. Cut into wedges to serve.

Makes 6 to 8 servings

Meat Crust Pie

Cheesy Rice Casserole

2 cups hot cooked rice
1 1/3 cups *French's*® French Fried Onions, divided
1 cup sour cream
1 jar (16 ounces) medium salsa
1 cup (4 ounces) shredded Cheddar or taco blend cheese

Microwave Directions
Combine rice and 2/3 cup French Fried Onions in bowl. Spoon half of the rice mixture into microwavable 2-quart shallow casserole. Spread sour cream over rice mixture.

Layer half of the salsa and half of the cheese over sour cream. Sprinkle with remaining rice mixture, salsa and cheese. Cover loosely with plastic wrap. Microwave on HIGH 8 minutes or until heated through. Sprinkle with remaining 2/3 cup onions. Microwave 1 minute or until onions are golden brown. *Makes 6 servings*

Prep Time: 15 minutes ✦ Cook Time: 9 minutes

Ham with Spring Vegetables

1 can (10 3/4 ounces) condensed cream of celery soup, undiluted
3/4 cup uncooked rice
1 tablespoon butter or margarine
1 to 1 1/2 pounds HILLSHIRE FARM® Ham, cut into bite-size pieces
1 package (10 ounces) frozen mixed vegetables
1 can (4 ounces) sliced mushrooms, drained
1 cup (4 ounces) shredded Swiss cheese

Preheat oven to 350°F.

Combine soup, rice, 3/4 cup water and butter in large skillet over medium heat. Bring mixture to a boil; reduce heat and simmer 5 minutes. Combine rice mixture with Ham, vegetables and mushrooms in medium casserole; sprinkle top with cheese. Bake, covered, 20 to 25 minutes or until rice is cooked. *Makes 4 servings*

Cheesy Rice Casserole

141

Herb-Baked Fish & Rice

1 ½ cups hot chicken broth

½ cup uncooked white rice

¼ teaspoon Italian seasoning

¼ teaspoon garlic powder

1 package (10 ounces) frozen chopped broccoli, thawed and drained

1 ⅓ cups *French's®* French Fried Onions, divided

1 tablespoon grated Parmesan cheese

1 pound unbreaded fish fillets, thawed if frozen

Paprika (optional)

½ cup (2 ounces) shredded Cheddar cheese

Preheat oven to 375°F. In 12×8-inch baking dish, combine broth, uncooked rice and seasonings. Bake, covered, at 375°F for 10 minutes. Top with broccoli, ⅔ cup French Fried Onions and Parmesan cheese. Place fish fillets diagonally down center of dish; sprinkle fish lightly with paprika. Bake, covered, at 375°F for 20 to 25 minutes or until fish flakes easily with fork. Stir rice. Top fish with Cheddar cheese and remaining ⅔ cup French Fried Onions; bake, uncovered, 3 minutes or until onions are golden brown.   *Makes 3 to 4 servings*

Microwave Directions: In 12×8-inch microwave-safe dish, prepare rice mixture as above, except reduce broth to 1 ¼ cups. Cook, covered, on HIGH 5 minutes, stirring halfway through cooking time. Stir in broccoli, ⅔ cup onions and Parmesan cheese. Arrange fish fillets in single layer on top of rice mixture; sprinkle fish lightly with paprika. Cook, covered, on MEDIUM (50-60%) 18 to 20 minutes or until fish flakes easily with fork and rice is done. Rotate dish halfway through cooking time. Top fish with Cheddar cheese and remaining ⅔ *cup* onions; cook, uncovered, on HIGH 1 minute or until cheese melts. Let stand 5 minutes.

Herb-Baked Fish & Rice

Italian Sausage Supper

1 pound mild Italian sausage, casing removed
1 cup chopped onion
3 medium zucchini, sliced (about 1 ½ cups)
1 can (6 ounces) CONTADINA® Tomato Paste
1 cup water
1 teaspoon dried basil leaves, crushed
½ teaspoon salt
3 cups cooked rice
1 cup (4 ounces) shredded mozzarella cheese
¼ cup (1 ounce) grated Romano cheese

1. Brown sausage with onion in large skillet, stirring to break up sausage; drain, reserving 1 tablespoon drippings.

2. Spoon sausage mixture into greased 2-quart casserole dish. Add zucchini to skillet; sauté for 5 minutes or until crisp-tender.

3. Combine tomato paste, water, basil and salt in medium bowl. Stir in rice. Spoon over sausage mixture. Arrange zucchini slices on top; sprinkle with mozzarella and Romano cheeses.

4. Cover. Bake in preheated 350°F oven for 20 minutes.   *Makes 6 servings*

Prep Time: 18 minutes ✦ Cook Time: 20 minutes

Italian Sausage Supper

Turkey and Rice Quiche

3 cups cooked rice, cooled to room temperature

1 $^1/_2$ cups chopped cooked turkey

1 medium tomato, seeded and finely diced

$^1/_4$ cup sliced green onions

$^1/_4$ cup finely diced green bell pepper

1 tablespoon chopped fresh basil *or* 1 teaspoon dried basil leaves

$^1/_2$ teaspoon seasoned salt

$^1/_8$ to $^1/_4$ teaspoon ground red pepper

$^1/_2$ cup skim milk

3 eggs, beaten

Vegetable cooking spray

$^1/_2$ cup **(2 ounces)** shredded Cheddar cheese

$^1/_2$ cup **(2 ounces)** shredded mozzarella cheese

Combine rice, turkey, tomato, green onions, bell pepper, basil, salt, red pepper, milk and eggs in 13×9×2-inch pan coated with cooking spray. Top with cheeses. Bake at 375°F for 20 minutes or until knife inserted near center comes out clean. To serve, cut quiche into 8 squares. *Makes 8 servings*

Favorite recipe from **USA Rice**

Turkey and Rice Quiche

Family-Style Frankfurters with Rice and Red Beans

1 tablespoon vegetable oil

1 medium onion, chopped

1/2 medium green bell pepper, chopped

2 cloves garlic, minced

1 can (14 ounces) red kidney beans, rinsed and drained

1 can (14 ounces) Great Northern beans, rinsed and drained

1/2 pound beef frankfurters, cut into 1/4-inch-thick pieces

1 cup uncooked instant brown rice

1 cup vegetable broth

1/4 cup packed brown sugar

1/4 cup ketchup

3 tablespoons dark molasses

1 tablespoon Dijon mustard

1. Preheat oven to 350°F. Spray 13×9-inch baking dish with nonstick cooking spray.

2. Heat oil in Dutch oven over medium-high heat until hot. Add onion, bell pepper and garlic; cook and stir 2 minutes or until onion is tender.

3. Add beans, frankfurters, rice, broth, brown sugar, ketchup, molasses and mustard to vegetables; stir to blend. Transfer to prepared dish.

4. Cover tightly with foil and bake 30 minutes or until rice is tender.

Makes 6 servings

Family-Style Frankfurters with Rice and Red Beans

Zesty Italian Stuffed Peppers

3 bell peppers (green, red or yellow)
1 pound ground beef
1 jar (14 ounces) spaghetti sauce
1 1/3 cups *French's*® French Fried Onions, divided
2 tablespoons *Frank's*® *RedHot*® Original Cayenne Pepper Sauce
1/2 cup uncooked instant rice
1/4 cup sliced ripe olives
1 cup (4 ounces) shredded mozzarella cheese

Preheat oven to 400°F. Cut bell peppers in half lengthwise through stems; discard seeds. Place pepper halves, cut sides up, in shallow 2-quart baking dish; set aside.

Place beef in large microwavable bowl. Microwave on HIGH 5 minutes or until meat is browned, stirring once. Drain. Stir in spaghetti sauce, 2/3 cup French Fried Onions, *Frank's RedHot* Sauce, rice and olives. Spoon evenly into bell pepper halves.

Cover; bake 35 minutes or until bell peppers are tender. Uncover; sprinkle with cheese and remaining 2/3 cup onions. Bake 1 minute or until onions are golden brown.

Makes 6 servings

Prep Time: 10 minutes ✦ **Cook Time:** 36 minutes

Hot Tip

Store unwashed sweet bell peppers in the refrigerator. Green peppers begin to lose their crispness after three to four days, red and yellow peppers are even more perishable.

Zesty Italian Stuffed Pepper

Teriyaki Chicken Medley

2 cups cooked white rice (about ¾ cup uncooked)
2 cups (10 ounces) cooked chicken, cut into strips
1 ⅓ cups *French's*® French Fried Onions, divided
1 package (12 ounces) frozen bell pepper strips, thawed and drained*
1 jar (12 ounces) chicken gravy
3 tablespoons teriyaki sauce

Or, substitute 2 cups sliced bell peppers for frozen pepper strips.

Preheat oven to 400°F. Grease 2-quart oblong baking dish. Press rice onto bottom of prepared dish.

Combine chicken, ⅔ cup French Fried Onions, bell pepper strips, gravy and teriyaki sauce in large bowl; mix well. Pour mixture over rice layer. Cover; bake 30 minutes or until heated through. Top with remaining ⅔ cup onions. Bake 1 minute or until onions are golden brown. *Makes 4 to 6 servings*

Prep Time: 10 minutes ✦ **Cook Time:** 31 minutes

152

SPAM® and Rice Casserole

1 (12-ounce) can SPAM® Classic, cubed
2 cups cooked white rice
½ cup *each* chopped water chestnuts and sliced celery
¼ cup sliced green onions
¼ teaspoon black pepper
1 (10¾-ounce) can condensed cream of mushroom soup, undiluted
⅓ cup mayonnaise or salad dressing

Heat oven to 350°F. In medium bowl, combine SPAM®, rice, water chestnuts, celery, green onions and pepper. In small bowl, combine soup and mayonnaise; mix with SPAM® mixture. Spoon into 1½-quart casserole. Bake 35 to 40 minutes or until thoroughly heated. *Makes 4 to 6 servings*

Teriyaki Chicken Medley

Acknowledgments

The publisher would like to thank the companies and organizations listed below for the use of their recipes and photographs in this publication.

BelGioioso® Cheese, Inc.

Birds Eye® Foods

Bob Evans®

Crisco is a registered trademark of The J.M. Smucker Company

Del Monte Corporation

Florida Department of Agriculture and Consumer Services, Bureau of Seafood and Aquaculture

Hebrew National®

Heinz North America

The Hidden Valley® Food Products Company

Hillshire Farm®

Hormel Foods, LLC

Jennie-O Turkey Store®

Mrs. Dash®

National Turkey Federation

Nestlé USA

North Dakota Beef Commission

Reckitt Benckiser Inc.

Smucker's® trademark of The J.M. Smucker Company

StarKist Seafood Company

Unilever Foods North America

USA Rice Federation

Veg•All®

VOLUME MEASUREMENTS (dry)

$\frac{1}{8}$ teaspoon = 0.5 mL
$\frac{1}{4}$ teaspoon = 1 mL
$\frac{1}{2}$ teaspoon = 2 mL
$\frac{3}{4}$ teaspoon = 4 mL
1 teaspoon = 5 mL
1 tablespoon = 15 mL
2 tablespoons = 30 mL
$\frac{1}{4}$ cup = 60 mL
$\frac{1}{3}$ cup = 75 mL
$\frac{1}{2}$ cup = 125 mL
$\frac{2}{3}$ cup = 150 mL
$\frac{3}{4}$ cup = 175 mL
1 cup = 250 mL
2 cups = 1 pint = 500 mL
3 cups = 750 mL
4 cups = 1 quart = 1 L

VOLUME MEASUREMENTS (fluid)

1 fluid ounce (2 tablespoons) = 30 mL
4 fluid ounces ($\frac{1}{2}$ cup) = 125 mL
8 fluid ounces (1 cup) = 250 mL
12 fluid ounces ($1\frac{1}{2}$ cups) = 375 mL
16 fluid ounces (2 cups) = 500 mL

WEIGHTS (mass)

$\frac{1}{2}$ ounce = 15 g
1 ounce = 30 g
3 ounces = 90 g
4 ounces = 120 g
8 ounces = 225 g
10 ounces = 285 g
12 ounces = 360 g
16 ounces = 1 pound = 450 g

DIMENSIONS

$\frac{1}{16}$ inch = 2 mm
$\frac{1}{8}$ inch = 3 mm
$\frac{1}{4}$ inch = 6 mm
$\frac{1}{2}$ inch = 1.5 cm
$\frac{3}{4}$ inch = 2 cm
1 inch = 2.5 cm

OVEN TEMPERATURES

250°F = 120°C
275°F = 140°C
300°F = 150°C
325°F = 160°C
350°F = 180°C
375°F = 190°C
400°F = 200°C
425°F = 220°C
450°F = 230°C

BAKING PAN SIZES

Utensil	Size in Inches/Quarts	Metric Volume	Size in Centimeters
Baking or Cake Pan (square or rectangular)	8×8×2	2 L	20×20×5
	9×9×2	2.5 L	23×23×5
	12×8×2	3 L	30×20×5
	13×9×2	3.5 L	33×23×5
Loaf Pan	8×4×3	1.5 L	20×10×7
	9×5×3	2 L	23×13×7
Round Layer Cake Pan	8×1½	1.2 L	20×4
	9×1½	1.5 L	23×4
Pie Plate	8×1¼	750 mL	20×3
	9×1¼	1 L	23×3
Baking Dish or Casserole	1 quart	1 L	—
	1½ quart	1.5 L	—
	2 quart	2 L	—